GODSON S

LEARN THE BASICS AND START SMART

Table of Contents

Complete Guide
To
Mastering The Markets

;;;kThe Complete Guide to Mastering the Markets

This is a work of non-fiction. While every effort has been made to ensure the accuracy of information presented herein, the author and publisher make no warranties regarding the completeness or reliability of the content.

Trading and investing involve risk, and readers should consult a qualified financial advisor before making investment decisions.

The author will not be held responsible for any losses or damages resulting from the use of this material.

Published by:

Godson Publications

India

First Edition: 2025

Cover Design: Godson

Editor: Godson

Chapter 1

What Is Trading?

Introduction: The Power Behind Every Trade

Imagine standing in a busy marketplace. People are shouting prices, exchanging money, and negotiating deals. One person sells apples, another buys them both walk away satisfied. This simple act of exchange is the foundation of **trading**.

Trading is not new. It has existed for thousands of years from ancient barter systems to modern online stock markets. But today, trading has evolved into something far more powerful.

With just a smartphone and internet connection, anyone can participate in the world's biggest markets stocks, forex, commodities, and even cryptocurrencies.

Trading is more than buying and selling; it's about **understanding value, timing, and opportunity**. It's about making smart decisions that can change your financial future.

This chapter will introduce you to what trading really means, how it works, and why it can be one of the most exciting and life-changing skills you can ever learn.

1.1 Understanding the Meaning of Trading

At its core, **trading means exchanging one thing of value for another**. In the financial world, trading usually means **buying and selling financial assets** such as shares, currencies, or commodities with the aim of making a profit.

Let's take an example:

You buy a company's stock at ₹100. A few weeks later, its price rises to ₹120. You sell it. Your profit is ₹20 per share. That's trading in its simplest form **buy low, sell high**.

Trading is not gambling. It's not luck. Successful traders don't guess; they **analyze, plan, and manage risk**.

The goal of a trader is to use logic, strategy, and discipline to find opportunities in the market and take advantage of price movements.

1.2 The Evolution of Trading: From Barter to Digital Markets

The story of trading begins long before computers existed.

In ancient times, people exchanged goods directly wheat for salt, gold for spices, or cattle for grain. This was called the **barter system.**

Then came **money**, which changed everything. Coins and currency made it easier to store and measure value. Markets began to form places where people met to trade goods and services.

Fast forward to the 17th century:

The first **stock exchange** was created in Amsterdam. People could buy small "shares" of trading companies a revolutionary idea that allowed ordinary people to invest and earn profits.

Today, trading has gone digital. You don't need to visit a market or talk to a broker face-to-face. Everything happens electronically millions of trades every second across global markets.

From gold to Google, from spices to stocks trading has always been a symbol of **human progress.**

1.3 The Two Worlds: Investing vs. Trading

Many people confuse **trading** with **investing**, but they are not the same.

Feature	Trading	Investing
Time Frame	Short-term (minutes to months)	Long-term (years to decades)
Goal	Quick profits from price movement	Building wealth over time
Focus	Market timing	Company fundamentals
Risk	Higher (more market exposure)	Lower (if diversified)

An **investor** buys and holds assets for a long period, waiting for them to grow in value.

A **trader**, on the other hand, looks for shorter-term opportunities.

For example, an investor may buy Apple stock and hold it for 10 years. A trader may buy and sell it several times within a week, profiting from small price changes.

Both can make money but the mindset and methods are very different.

Trading is **active**. Investing is **patient**. Both are powerful in their own way.

1.4 Types of Trading

Trading can be done in many ways depending on how long you hold your position and what your strategy is.

1. **Intraday Trading** – Buying and selling within the same day. No positions are held overnight.
   Example: You buy 100 shares in the morning and sell them by afternoon.
   Goal: Profit from small daily price movements.
2. **Swing Trading** – Holding a trade for several days or weeks.
   Goal: Capture medium-term trends.
3. **Positional Trading** – Holding trades for months.
   Goal: Benefit from large market moves.
4. **Scalping** – Ultra-short-term trading.
   Goal: Make many tiny profits throughout the day.

Each style needs different levels of time, focus, and risk tolerance. Beginners often start with **swing trading** or **positional trading**, as they're easier to manage.

1.5 Why People Trade

Trading attracts people for many reasons money, freedom, challenge, or passion.

Here are some key motivations:

- **Financial Independence:** You can earn without depending on a salary or boss.
- **Flexibility:** You can trade from anywhere with an internet connection.
- **Unlimited Potential:** There's no fixed income your skill determines

your success.

- **Thrill of Learning:** Markets are dynamic and exciting.

But trading also comes with risk. Prices can go against you, and losses are part of the journey. That's why education and discipline are crucial.

As the saying goes:

"Trading gives you freedom but only if you earn it with patience and knowledge."

1.6 The Market: Where Trading Happens

When you buy or sell an asset, you're doing it in a **market**.

A market is simply a place physical or digital where buyers and sellers meet.

The major financial markets are:

1. **Stock Market:** For shares of companies (e.g., NSE, BSE, NYSE).
2. **Forex Market:** For currencies (e.g., USD/INR, EUR/USD).
3. **Commodity Market:** For gold, silver, oil, etc.
4. **Crypto Market:** For digital currencies like Bitcoin, Ethereum.

Each market has its own timing, rules, and risks.

But the basic principle is always the same **supply and demand**. When demand is high, prices rise; when supply is high, prices fall.

Understanding this simple rule is the first step to becoming a good trader.

1.7 How Trading Works

Let's break down a simple trade:

1. You open a trading account with a broker.
2. You analyze the market and find a stock to buy.
3. You place an order say 10 shares of Company A at ₹200.
4. The order is matched instantly on the exchange.
5. If the price goes up to ₹220 and you sell your profit is ₹200.

That's the mechanical part. But the **real challenge** lies in predicting whether prices will go up or down.

That's where **technical analysis**, **fundamental analysis**, and **market psychology** come in all of which you'll learn in later chapters.

1.8 The Players in the Market

Every trade has two sides a **buyer** and a **seller**.
But behind them are different types of participants:

- **Retail Traders:** Ordinary individuals like you and me.
- **Institutional Traders:** Banks, hedge funds, mutual funds.
- **Market Makers:** Companies that ensure liquidity by buying/selling continuously.
- **Brokers:** The middlemen who connect you to the market.

Each player affects market behavior in a unique way. Understanding who moves the market helps you make smarter trades.

1.9 Emotions and Mindset in Trading

Trading is not just numbers and charts it's a **mental game**.
Two emotions dominate every trader:

- **Fear** – fear of losing money or missing out.
- **Greed** – wanting more profit and refusing to stop.

The most successful traders are those who control both. They follow rules, not emotions.

"The market rewards discipline, not desire."

As a beginner, you'll often feel emotional highs and lows. But with time, you'll learn to trade with **logic, not feelings**.

1.10 The Importance of Education and Practice

You wouldn't fly a plane without training so why trade without learning?
Before risking real money, study the basics:

- Learn how markets move.
- Understand charts and patterns.
- Practice in demo accounts.

Knowledge is your best protection.

Many new traders lose money because they skip this step. They rush into live trading without preparation and the market punishes impatience.

Remember:

"Trading is not a race; it's a lifelong skill."

1.11 The Risks of Trading

Every opportunity has a cost. Trading can offer great rewards, but it also carries risks.

Some common risks are:

- **Market Risk:** Prices move unexpectedly.
- **Emotional Risk:** Poor decisions made under pressure.
- **System Risk:** Technical issues like app crashes.
- **Leverage Risk:** Borrowing money to trade can multiply losses.

You can't avoid risk but you can **manage it**.

That's what separates beginners from professionals.

1.12 Trading Myths You Should Forget

There are many myths about trading. Let's break a few:

1. **"Trading is gambling."** Wrong.

Gambling is luck-based; trading is knowledge-based.

1. **"You can get rich overnight."** Wrong.

Success comes from consistent effort.

1. **"You need a lot of money to start."** Wrong.

You can start small and grow slowly.

1. **"Only experts can trade."** Wrong.

Anyone can learn with patience and discipline.

1.13 Building the Foundation

Before placing your first trade, build your base:

- Set your goals *(Why are you trading?)*
- Choose your market *(Stocks? Crypto? Forex?)*
- Learn the tools *(Charts, indicators, apps)*
- Plan your risk *(How much can you afford to lose?)*

Trading is a business treat it like one. Keep records, study your results, and never stop learning.

1.14 A Glimpse Into the Trader's Life

A professional trader's day doesn't start with random buying and selling. It begins with:

- Reading global news
- Checking charts
- Reviewing past trades
- Planning new entries and exits

Trading requires discipline, patience, and structure. It's not about being on your phone all day it's about **making smart moves** at the right time.

1.15 The Future of Trading

Technology is transforming trading. Artificial intelligence, algorithms, and automation are now common tools.

But one thing will never change **human decision-making**.

No software can replace your ability to think, adapt, and learn. In the future, traders who combine knowledge with technology will lead the game.

1.16 Summary: The First Step Toward Mastery

Trading is not magic. It's a skill one that anyone can learn with time and effort.

You've now learned:

- What trading means
- How markets work

- The difference between trading and investing
- Why emotions and risk management matter

As you move to the next chapters, remember:
Every professional trader once started as a beginner just like you.
"The market is not your enemy. It's your teacher."

Chapter 2

How the Market Works

Introduction: The Invisible Engine of the Economy

Every day, billions of dollars move across the world stocks change hands, currencies are exchanged, and commodities are traded. Behind all this activity lies a fascinating system called **the market**.

The market is like the heartbeat of the global economy. It connects people who have money with people who need money, buyers with sellers, and dreams with opportunities.

But how does this system actually work? Who sets the prices? Why do markets rise and fall? Why does one stock suddenly boom while another crashes?

Understanding **how the market works** is the foundation of every successful trader's journey. Without this knowledge, trading is like sailing a ship without a compass you might move, but you'll never know where you're going.

2.1 What Is a Market?

In simple terms, a **market** is a place physical or digital where people come together to **buy and sell.**

It could be a vegetable market in your local town or a global stock exchange in New York. The concept is the same: an environment where goods, services, or financial instruments are exchanged for money.

When we talk about trading, we usually mean **financial market** places where assets like shares, currencies, or commodities are traded.

These markets are not run by a single person or organization. Instead, they are **networks of millions of participants** interacting through technology and information.

The beauty of a market is its simplicity buyers want to pay the lowest price, and sellers want to receive the highest price. The point where both agree is called the **market price.**

2.2 The Core Principle: Supply and Demand

At the heart of every market is one timeless rule:

Prices are determined by supply and demand.

- **Supply** means how much of something is available.
- **Demand** means how much people want it.

When demand is greater than supply, prices rise.

When supply is greater than demand, prices fall.

Example:

If everyone wants to buy shares of Company A but only a few are available, the price will go up.

If nobody wants them and sellers are desperate to sell, the price will go down.

This balance between supply and demand keeps the market alive constantly moving, constantly changing. Every second, millions of buy and sell orders fight for dominance. The result is what we call **price movement.**

2.3 The Players in the Market

Every market has different types of participants. Understanding who they are and how they behave gives you an edge as a trader.

1. **Retail Traders:**
   Individuals like you and me who trade using online platforms. They form a large part of the market but usually hold smaller positions.
2. **Institutional Investors:**
   Big players banks, hedge funds, insurance companies, and mutual funds. They move huge amounts of money and can influence prices.
3. **Market Makers:**
   These are specialized firms that buy and sell continuously to provide liquidity (so that buyers and sellers can always find each other).
4. **Brokers:**
   The middlemen who connect traders to exchanges. They provide trading apps, platforms, and customer support.
5. **Regulators:**
   Organizations like **SEBI** (India), **SEC** (USA), or **FCA** (UK) that make sure the market is fair, transparent, and not manipulated.

Each of these players has a purpose. Retail traders look for opportunity, institutions look for growth, and regulators ensure order. Together, they form a complex but efficient ecosystem.

2.4 Types of Financial Markets

Financial markets come in many forms. Each one serves a different purpose and trades different kinds of assets.

1. Stock Market

The most well-known type. Here, you can buy and sell **shares** ownership pieces of companies.

For example, if you buy one share of TCS or Apple, you become a part-owner of that company.

2. Forex Market

This is the **foreign exchange market**, where currencies are traded. It's the largest market in the world, with a daily volume of over $6 trillion.

Here, you might trade USD/INR or EUR/USD pairs, trying to profit from changes in currency values.

3. Commodity Market

Gold, silver, crude oil, agricultural products all are traded here. Commodities often react to global events like wars, weather, and demand changes.

4. Derivatives Market

A more advanced market where people trade contracts based on the price of other assets (like futures and options).

Derivatives allow traders to speculate or hedge risk.

5. Crypto Market

The newest and the most volatile market. Cryptocurrencies like Bitcoin, Ethereum, and Solana are traded 24/7 on online exchanges. This market runs without a central authority it's completely decentralized.

Understanding these markets helps you choose where to focus. Each has its own rhythm, risk, and reward.

2.5 How Prices Move

Price movement is the lifeblood of trading. Without movement, there's no opportunity to profit.

But what makes prices move?

1. **News and Events:**
   Company results, government policies, global events all influence market prices.
   Example: A company announces high profits → its stock price rises.
2. **Investor Sentiment:**
   Markets are emotional. Fear and greed drive decisions. If people feel optimistic, they buy more; if they panic, they sell.
3. **Economic Indicators:**
   Data like inflation, GDP, interest rates, and unemployment affect overall market direction.
4. **Supply and Demand Shifts:**
   If everyone starts buying gold, the price naturally increases.
5. **Speculation:**
   Traders betting on future price movement can push prices temporarily up or down.

Price movement is like waves in the ocean. You can't control them but if you learn how they form, you can ride them.

2.6 The Structure of a Trade

To understand how a trade happens, let's follow the journey step-by-step.

1. **You decide to buy** a stock at a certain price.
2. **Your order goes** through your broker's trading platform to the exchange.
3. **The exchange matches** your order with someone who wants to sell.
4. Once both agree on price, **the trade is executed** instantly.
5. The transaction details are stored, and your portfolio gets updated.

All of this happens in fractions of a second thanks to modern technology and automation.

The key takeaway:

Every price you see on your screen is the result of countless trades happening in real time.

2.7 The Role of Stock Exchanges

Stock exchanges are the **marketplaces** where trading happens. In India, the main ones are the **NSE (National Stock Exchange)** and the **BSE (Bombay Stock Exchange)**.

In the U.S., it's the **NYSE (New York Stock Exchange)** and **NASDAQ**.

Exchanges ensure that:

- All trades are transparent.
- Buyers and sellers are protected.
- Prices are updated in real time.
- Rules and regulations are followed.

They act like referees keeping the game fair and balanced.

2.8 Market Hours and Timing

Unlike crypto markets that run 24/7, most financial markets have fixed hours.

- **Indian stock market:** 9:15 AM – 3:30 PM
- **Forex market:** 24 hours, Monday to Friday
- **Commodities market:** Usually 10 AM – 11:30 PM
- **Crypto market:** Open 24/7

Timing matters in trading.

Some traders focus on opening hours (when volume is high), while others prefer quieter periods for stability.

Knowing when to trade is just as important as knowing **what** to trade.

2.9 Bulls and Bears: The Market's Emotions

Markets are often described using two powerful animals: **Bull** and **Bear**.

- A **Bull Market** means prices are rising, optimism is high, and investors are confident.
- A **Bear Market** means prices are falling, fear dominates, and traders

are cautious.

These terms capture the psychology of the crowd.

The best traders learn to adapt to both to find opportunity whether the market is rising or falling.

"A trader doesn't fight the market; he flows with it."

2.10 Liquidity: The Market's Lifeblood

Liquidity means how easily you can buy or sell an asset without changing its price too much.

- If a stock is highly liquid, it means many people are trading it you can enter and exit anytime.
- If it's illiquid, few people are trading prices can jump sharply, and orders might take time to fill.

Traders prefer **liquid markets** because they offer speed, safety, and smoother price action.

2.11 The Role of Brokers and Technology

In the past, traders had to call their brokers to place orders. Today, you can trade from your phone in seconds.

Brokers act as your bridge to the market. They provide:

- Trading apps and platforms
- Market data and charts
- Analytical tools and research

Thanks to technology, even small traders now have access toi the same information as professionals.

That's the beauty of modern trading **knowledge has been democratized**.

2.12 The Economic Connection

Markets don't move in isolation. They are deeply connected to the **economy**.

When the economy grows, companies make more profits, and stock prices rise. When the economy slows, profits shrink, and prices fall.

Key economic drivers include:

- **Interest Rates:** Lower rates make borrowing cheaper → boosts markets.
- **Inflation:** High inflation reduces buying power → hurts markets.
- **Employment Levels:** More jobs = more spending = stronger markets.
- **Government Policy:** Taxes, trade deals, and budgets all have market impact.

By understanding the economy, you can understand why markets behave the way they do.

2.13 Market Cycles

Every market goes through **cycles** repeated phases of growth and decline.

1. **Accumulation Phase:** Smart investors quietly buy. Prices move slowly.
2. **Mark-Up Phase:** Public interest increases; prices rise quickly.
3. **Distribution Phase:** Big players start selling to the crowd.
4. **Mark-Down Phase:** Prices fall as optimism fades.

Recognizing these cycles helps you trade **with** the market, not against it.

2.14 The Role of Emotions in Market Movement

Markets reflect human emotions on a global scale.

- **Greed** drives prices up.
- **Fear** drags them down.

Even large institutions are affected by emotion it's what makes markets unpredictable at times. A trader's job is to understand this emotional rhythm and use it wisely.

2.15 How Traders Profit From the Market

There are two main ways to make money from price movement:

1. **Going Long:**
   Buying first, selling later when price rises.
   (Example: Buy at ₹100, sell at ₹120 profit ₹20.)
2. **Going Short:**
   Selling first, buying later when price falls.
   (Example: Sell at ₹120, buy back at ₹100 profit ₹20.)

Short selling allows traders to make money even in falling markets a powerful concept once you understand it.

2.16 The Importance of Volume

Volume means how many shares or contracts are traded in a given time.

- High volume means strong interest and confirmation of price moves.
- Low volume means weak conviction.

Always remember:

"Price tells you what is happening.
Volume tells you how strong it is."

2.17 Market Efficiency and Randomness

Markets are mostly efficient meaning prices reflect all available information. But not always. Human behavior, rumours, and overreactions create **inefficiencies** short-term opportunities that skilled traders can exploit.

That's where technical analysis comes in a system to read price patterns and predict future movement.

2.18 Global Interconnection

Today's markets are **interconnected.**

A decision made by the U.S. Federal Reserve can move prices in India, Japan, or Europe within minutes.

Oil prices, global conflicts, or natural disasters all ripple through the system instantly. As a trader, you must think globally but act locally.

2.19 Technology, Algorithms, and the Future

Modern trading is dominated by algorithms computer programs that execute trades in milliseconds. They follow rules, patterns, and mathematical models.

While humans still set the strategies, machines now perform most of the execution. This has made markets faster, more efficient, but also more competitive.

The future will blend human intelligence with artificial intelligence traders who can adapt will thrive.

2.20 Summary: The Market Is a Living Organism

The market is not just numbers and charts it's **alive**. It breathes, moves, and reacts to the emotions, hopes, and fears of millions of people.

You've now learned:

- What markets are and how they function
- Who participates and how prices are set
- Why emotions, economics, and technology shape the market's rhythm

As you move ahead, remember:
"You can't control the market, but you can control how you react to it."

Chapter 3

Types of Trading

Introduction: Many Roads, One Destination

There are many each with its own speed, rhythm, and strategy. Some traders hold positions for months, others for seconds. Some study charts, others study news. Yet they all share the same goal: **to make consistent profit from price movement.**

Just like in sports cricket, football, tennis the rules differ, but the spirit of competition remains the same. Trading is no different. Your job is to find which "game" suits your style, your patience, and your mindset.

This chapter explores the **major types of trading**, how each one works, and which might be right for you. Whether you want fast action or steady growth, you'll find your trading identity here.

3.1 Understanding the Time Factor

The biggest difference between trading types is **time** how long you hold your position.

Time decides:

- How much risk you take
- How many trades you make
- How emotionally demanding it is

In general, there are **four main categories**:

1. **Scalping** – trades last seconds or minutes.
2. **Intraday Trading** – trades last within a single day.
3. **Swing Trading** – trades last for days or weeks.
4. **Positional Trading** – trades last for months or even years.

Let's explore each of them deeply.

3.2 Scalping: The Art of Speed

Scalping is the **fastest form of trading**. Scalpers open and close dozens (sometimes hundreds) of trades in a single day, aiming for **tiny profits** often just a few paise or cents per trade.

Imagine a surfer catching every small wave. That's what a scalper does jumping in and out before the wave breaks.

How It Works

- Scalpers use **1-minute or 5-minute charts.**
- They rely on **technical indicators** like Moving Averages and Volume.
- They target **small price changes** (for example, ₹1–₹2 per share).

Because they trade frequently, **speed and discipline** are everything.

Advantages

- Many opportunities every day.
- Small market moves can bring profit.
- Little overnight risk (positions closed quickly).

Disadvantages

- Emotionally exhausting.
- Requires fast internet and instant execution.
- Brokerage and transaction costs can reduce profit.

Who It Suits

People who love **fast decision-making** and can stay calm under pressure.

"Scalping is not about chasing profit it's about mastering precision."

3.3 Intraday Trading: The Daily Challenge

Intraday (or day trading) is the most **popular** form among beginners. You buy and sell within the same trading day no positions carried overnight.

For example:

- You buy 100 shares of Infosys at ₹1,500 in the morning.
- By afternoon, the price rises to ₹1,525.
- You sell and book ₹2,500 profit before market close.

Simple, right? But behind every intraday success lies analysis, timing, and emotion control.

How It Works

- Uses **5-minute to 1-hour charts.**
- Traders identify daily trends or breakouts.
- Common strategies: support/resistance, volume breakouts, moving average crossovers.

Advantages

- Daily profit potential.
- No overnight risk (market closes, so price can't gap overnight).
- Quick learning cycle you see results immediately.

Disadvantages

- High emotional stress.
- Requires continuous screen time.
- Market volatility can trigger quick losses.

Who It Suits

People with time, focus, and patience to monitor the market for hours.

"Day trading teaches patience, not speed. Wait for the right moment, then strike."

3.4 Swing Trading: The Middle Path

If intraday trading feels too fast and positional trading feels too slow, **swing trading** is the perfect balance.

Swing traders hold positions for **a few days to a few weeks**. Their goal is to capture **short- to medium-term price movements** the "swings" between highs and lows.

For example:

- You buy Tata Motors at ₹800.
- Five days later, it reaches ₹860.

- You sell a ₹60 profit per share.

Swing traders combine **technical analysis** with a bit of **fundamental awareness.**

How It Works

- Uses **1-hour to daily charts.**
- Trades often follow patterns like trendlines, channels, and moving averages.
- Common tools: RSI, MACD, Bollinger Bands.

Advantages

- Less stress you don't need to watch markets all day.
- Higher profit per trade than intraday.
- Can trade part-time while working or studying.

Disadvantages

- Overnight risk prices may gap due to news/events.
- Requires patience to hold through small pullbacks.

Who It Suits

Beginners who want to trade calmly and learn the rhythm of the market.

"Swing trading is like fishing cast your line, wait patiently, and pull when the moment is right."

3.5 Positional Trading: The Power of Patience

Positional trading is for those who think long-term.

Here, you hold trades for **weeks, months, or even years**, focusing on major market trends.

You don't worry about small daily fluctuations. Instead, you ride **big waves** of movement.

Example:

- You buy Reliance Industries at ₹2,200.
- Six months later, it reaches ₹2,800.
- You sell ₹600 profit per share.

How It Works

- Uses **daily, weekly, or monthly charts.**
- Focuses more on **fundamental factors** (company earnings, economy, policy).
- Less frequent trades quality over quantity.

Advantages

- Requires minimal time commitment.
- Lower emotional stress.
- Larger potential profits per trade.

Disadvantages

- Requires capital and patience.
- Long holding period means exposure to market risks.

Who It Suits

Traders who prefer calm, logic-driven decision-making not constant action.
"The market rewards patience more than perfection."

3.6 Comparing the Four Types

Type	Duration	Effort	Profit per Trade	Risk	Ideal For
Scalping	Seconds -Minutes	Very High	Very Small	High	Speed Lovers
Intraday	Same Day	High	Moderate	Medium–High	Active Traders
Swing	Days -Weeks	Medium	Good	Medium	Beginners & Part timers
Positional	Weeks–Months	Low	High	Medium	Long-term Thinkers

Choosing your style isn't about right or wrong it's about **fit**.

If you love fast action, intraday might suit you.

If you prefer calm, swing or positional trading is ideal.

3.7 Other Trading Styles

Apart from the main four, there are some special types of trading that use different philosophies.

1. Algorithmic Trading

Also called **Algo trading**, it uses computer programs to execute trades automatically. These algorithms follow predefined rules like price, time, or volume. Used mostly by institutions and professionals.

2. News-Based Trading

Some traders focus on **breaking news** company results, government policies, or global events. They trade based on market reactions to information.

3. High-Frequency Trading (HFT)

An advanced form of algo trading where trades happen in microseconds. Mostly dominated by large firms with advanced technology.

4. Copy Trading

Beginners can automatically **copy** the trades of experienced professionals using online platforms. It's a good learning tool but requires careful selection of reliable traders.

3.8 Choosing the Right Type for You

Your trading type should match your **personality, time, and mindset.**

Ask yourself:

- How much time can I spend trading daily?
- Do I prefer quick results or steady growth?
- Can I handle stress and fast decisions?
- Am I more technical or analytical?

Here's a simple guide:

If You Are...	Try This Type
Busy student or working professional	Swing / Positional Trading
Fast thinker, love excitement	Intraday / Scalping
Patient and analytical	Positional Trading
Data-driven and tech lover	Algorithmic / Copy Trading

Remember: You can experiment, but never mix all at once.

Focus on mastering one style then adapt over time.

"Trading success doesn't come from doing everything; it comes from doing one thing well."

3.9 The Role of Strategy

Every type of trading requires a **strategy** a set of rules for entry, exit, and risk.

For example:

- A **scalper's strategy** may focus on breakouts and volume spikes.
- A **swing trader's strategy** may use moving average crossovers.
- A **positional trader's strategy** may rely on fundamental analysis.

No matter the type, a good strategy includes:

1. Entry conditions *(when to buy)*
2. Exit conditions *(when to sell)*
3. Stop-loss *(how to protect yourself)*
4. Risk-reward ratio *(is the trade worth it?)*

Without a plan, even the best type of trading will fail.

3.10 Time Commitment and Lifestyle

Trading style also affects your **lifestyle**.

- **Scalpers** need full-time focus, fast reflexes, and high energy.
- **Intraday traders** spend 4–6 hours daily watching markets.
- **Swing traders** check markets once or twice a day.
- **Positional traders** spend only a few hours weekly.

Your time availability determines your style more than your ambition.

If you choose a type that doesn't match your routine, frustration follows. Trading should **fit into your life**, not consume it.

3.11 Risk in Each Type

Each trading type carries unique risks:

- **Scalping:** Execution errors, high transaction costs.
- **Intraday:** Sudden intraday volatility.
- **Swing:** Overnight gaps due to news.
- **Positional:** Long exposure to major events.

Risk can't be avoided but it can be **controlled** through stop losses and position sizing.

The more time you hold a position, the more you must respect uncertainty.

3.12 Building Experience Through Experimentation

You won't know your ideal style on day one. It takes **trial and error**. Try paper trading (demo mode) in each type for a few weeks.

Note which feels most natural, least stressful, and most consistent. That's your style. Once you find it **focus deeply** and master it.

3.13 The Psychological Difference

Each trading type also tests different parts of your psychology.

Type	Emotion Tested
Scalping	Pressure & speed
Intraday	Patience & focus
Swing	Discipline & confidence
Positional	Faith & conviction

That's why trading isn't just a financial game it's an **emotional journey**.

The best traders aren't those who find the perfect strategy they're those who understand their own minds.

3.14 Combining Styles

As you grow, you may combine styles strategically.

For example:

- Use **positional trades** for long-term growth.
- Add **swing trades** for mid-term income.
- Do light **intraday trading** for practice.

But balance is key. Overtrading leads to burnout.

Always protect your capital and your peace of mind.

3.15 How Professional Traders Choose

Professional traders don't choose based on excitement; they choose based on **edge** their proven advantage.

They analyze:

- Market volatility
- Personal schedule
- Risk tolerance
- Capital size

Then they design a style that **amplifies their strengths** and **minimizes their weaknesses**. That's why consistency matters more than frequency.

"Professionals don't trade more they trade better."

3.16 Adapting to Market Conditions

Markets change.

During high volatility, **intraday** or **scalping** might perform better.

During slow trends, **swing** or **positional** trading might be safer.

A flexible trader knows how to **adapt** without abandoning discipline.

3.17 Tools and Timeframes

Different types of trading use different **timeframes** and **tools**:

Type	Chart Timeframe	Main Tools
Scalping	1-min, 5-min	Volume, Moving Averages
Intraday	5-min, 15-min, 1-hr	RSI, MACD, VWAP
Swing	4-hr, Daily	Trendlines, Breakouts
Positional	Weekly, Monthly	Fundamentals, Patterns

The timeframe defines your trading world.

A scalper sees hundreds of candles per hour a positional trader may watch one chart per week. Choose the world where your mind feels calm.

3.18 The Evolution of a Trader

Most traders don't stick to one type forever. They evolve.

- Start with **swing trading** to learn patience and analysis.
- Move to **intraday** when you gain confidence.
- Later, explore **positional trading** for wealth building.

This natural evolution helps you understand markets from every angle.

In the end, your trading style becomes a reflection of your personality.

3.19 The Key to Success in Any Type

No matter what style you choose, these golden rules never change:

1. Always use a stop-loss.
2. Never risk more than you can afford to lose.
3. Trade with a plan not emotion.
4. Keep learning and adapting.
5. Focus on consistency, not quick profit.

Success in trading isn't about speed; it's about **discipline**.

"The market rewards patience, punishes greed, and respects preparation."

3.20 Summary: Find Your Rhythm

Trading offers many roads fast, slow, calm, or thrilling.
Each type has its own language, energy, and rhythm.
You've now learned:

- The four main types of trading and how they differ
- The pros and cons of each
- How to find which suits your personality
- The mindset and strategy behind every type

The journey ahead will teach you **how to use tools, read charts, and build your strategy** but before all that, you must remember one truth:

"The right type of trading isn't what makes money fastest.
It's the one you can follow consistently with confidence."

Chapter 4

Trading Instruments

Introduction: What You Actually Trade

Trading is not just a concept it is **action**. And action requires a tool, a vehicle, something tangible or digital that you buy and sell. These are called **trading instruments**.

Think of a painter: their instruments are brushes, paints, and canvas. Without them, creativity cannot take shape. Similarly, in trading, **instruments are the building blocks of your profits**.

In this chapter, we will explore the most common trading instruments what they are, how they work, and why traders choose them. Understanding these is crucial because every trading type (scalping, intraday, swing, positional) relies on these instruments to function.

Whether you dream of trading stocks, forex, commodities, or cryptocurrencies, mastering your instruments is the first step to mastering the market.

4.1 Stocks: Owning a Piece of a Company

A **stock** represents **ownership in a company**. When you buy one share, you own a small part of that company.

For example:

- Buying 10 shares of Infosys means you own a tiny portion of Infosys.
- If the company grows and earns profits, the stock price usually rises.
- You can then sell your shares for a profit.

Stocks are the most common trading instruments because:

- They are accessible to beginners
- They have high liquidity (easy to buy and sell)
- There is a wide variety of companies to choose from

How Stocks Make Money

1. **Capital Gains:** Selling at a higher price than purchase.
2. **Dividends:** A share of the company's profit paid to shareholders.

Key Points for Beginners

- Stocks are ideal for **long-term positional trading** and **swing trading**.
- Daily price fluctuations also allow **intraday trading**.
- Research is important: learn about the company's earnings, news, and fundamentals.

"Stocks are like seeds plant wisely, water patiently, and watch them grow."

4.2 Forex: Trading Currencies

The **Forex Market** (Foreign Exchange) is where **currencies are bought and sold**. It's the **largest financial market** in the world, with trillions of dollars traded every day.

Example:

- You exchange ₹80,000 for $1,000 when USD/INR is 80.
- If the rate moves to 82, your $1,000 is now worth ₹82,000.
- You earn ₹2,000 profit.

Why Forex Is Popular

- Open 24 hours, Monday to Friday
- Huge liquidity you can trade almost any time
- Offers leverage (trading with borrowed money), which can increase profits

Risks in Forex

- Currency fluctuations can be unpredictable
- Leverage magnifies both gains and losses

Who Trades Forex

- Professionals and retail traders alike

- People who want **fast-paced trading** or global market exposure

"In Forex, the world is your market and every currency tells a story."

4.3 Commodities: Tangible Wealth

Commodities are **physical goods** that are traded in financial markets. They include:

- **Metals:** gold, silver, platinum
- **Energy:** crude oil, natural gas
- **Agriculture:** wheat, sugar, coffee

Trading commodities allows you to **profit from changes in supply and demand**, often caused by global events, weather, or economic shifts.

Example:

- A drought reduces wheat supply → wheat prices rise → traders profit.
- Oil price increase affects gasoline prices → opportunity for energy traders.

Why Commodities Are Important

- Diversification: They behave differently from stocks and currencies
- Hedge against inflation: Physical assets like gold often rise when money loses value
- Opportunity for both short-term and long-term traders

Who Trades Commodities

- Swing traders love commodities for trend trading
- Positional traders use them for long-term wealth protection
- Professionals monitor global news and supply-demand factors

"Commodities remind traders that markets are connected to the real world."

4.4 Derivatives: Trading the Contract, Not the Asset

Derivatives are contracts whose value is based on the **price of another asset.** Common derivatives include **futures** and **options.**

Futures

A **future** is a contract to buy or sell an asset at a predetermined price on a specific date.

Example:

- You agree to buy 100 barrels of oil at $60 each in three months.
- If the price rises to $70 in three months, you profit $10 per barrel.

Options

An **option** gives the **right, but not the obligation** to buy or sell an asset at a set price.

- **Call Option:** Right to buy
- **Put Option:** Right to sell

Derivatives are powerful because they allow traders to:

- Hedge risk (protect against losses)
- Speculate on price movements without owning the asset

Risks in Derivatives

- Leverage increases risk you can lose more than your investment
- Requires skill and knowledge not recommended for complete beginners

"Derivatives are like advanced tools powerful in the right hands, dangerous in the wrong ones."

4.5 Cryptocurrencies: The Digital Frontier

Cryptocurrencies are **digital assets** that use **blockchain technology** for secure transactions. Bitcoin, Ethereum, and Solana are the most popular examples.

Why Crypto Is Exciting

- Open 24/7 trade anytime
- High volatility opportunity for fast profits
- Decentralized no single government controls them

Risks in Crypto

- Extreme price swings
- Security risks (hacks, scams)
- Regulatory uncertainty

Who Trades Crypto

- Intraday traders love volatility
- Swing traders profit from medium-term trends
- Positional traders invest in long-term adoption stories

"Crypto trading is like exploring a new world thrilling, unpredictable, and full of opportunity."

4.6 ETFs and Mutual Funds: Bundled Assets

Not everyone wants to pick individual stocks or commodities. **ETFs (Exchange-Traded Funds)** and **mutual funds** let you **invest in a basket of assets.**

- **ETF:** Trades like a stock on an exchange
- **Mutual Fund:** Professionally managed pool of investments

These instruments reduce risk through **diversification** and are ideal for beginners learning the market.

4.7 Bonds: Lending to Grow Wealth

A **bond** is essentially a loan to a government or company. You earn **interest** for lending your money.

- Low risk compared to stocks or crypto
- Fixed returns and predictable income
- Often used by positional traders as part of a balanced portfolio

"Bonds are the quiet, steady friends of a trader reliable and patient."

4.8 CFDs: Contract for Difference

CFDs allow traders to **speculate on price movement** without owning the underlying asset.

Example:

- You open a CFD to buy 100 shares of Infosys
- Price rises → you profit
- Price falls → you lose

CFDs are popular for leverage and flexibility but carry **high risk.**

4.9 Key Considerations When Choosing Instruments

When deciding what to trade, consider:

1. **Volatility:** More volatile instruments offer higher profit potential but higher risk.
2. **Liquidity:** High liquidity ensures smooth buying and selling.
3. **Timeframe:** Some instruments suit fast trades, others long-term.
4. **Knowledge:** Always trade what you understand.

"Choose your instruments like a musician chooses instruments the right one brings harmony to your strategy."

4.10 Combining Instruments for Strategy

Professional traders often **combine multiple instruments**:

- Hedge positions using derivatives
- Trade crypto for high risk, stocks for steady growth
- Use bonds for stability alongside equity trading

Diversification reduces risk and creates multiple profit opportunities.

4.11 Learning Curve and Practice

Start simple:

- Begin with **stocks or ETFs**
- Practice on **demo accounts**
- Slowly explore commodities, forex, crypto, and derivatives

Mastering instruments is **step-by-step** no rush.
"The instrument is just a tool; your skill turns it into profit."

4.12 The Psychological Aspect of Instruments

Each instrument tests your **patience, confidence, and strategy.**

- **High volatility instruments** (crypto, forex) test courage
- **Steady instruments** (bonds, ETFs) test patience
- **Complex instruments** (derivatives, CFDs) test discipline

Choose instruments that match your emotional strength as well as your financial goals.

4.13 The Role of Brokers and Platforms

Every instrument is traded via a **broker or trading platform.**
A good platform provides:

- Real-time quotes
- Easy order execution
- Risk management tools
- Research and news updates

Your choice of broker affects **speed, cost, and convenience.**

4.14 Risks Across Instruments

Every trading instrument carries risk:

- **Stocks:** Market swings
- **Forex:** Currency fluctuations
- **Commodities:** Supply-demand changes
- **Crypto:** Extreme volatility
- **Derivatives/CFDs:** Leverage magnifies loss
- **Bonds/ETFs:** Lower risk, slower growth

Understanding risk is more important than chasing profit.

4.15 The Key Takeaway

Trading instruments are **the vehicles of your trading journey**.

- **Stocks:** ownership and growth
- **Forex:** global currencies and opportunity
- **Commodities:** tangible goods, supply-demand swings
- **Derivatives:** contracts and leverage
- **Crypto:** digital frontier
- **Bonds/ETFs**: stability and diversification

Knowing the characteristics, risks, and advantages of each helps you **trade smarter**.

4.16 Summary: Tools of the Trader

Every trader must **choose their instruments wisely**. Your instruments define your strategy, timeframe, and profit potential.

As you move forward in this book, remember:

"Master the instruments first, and the market will follow."

You now have a solid understanding of **what can be traded, how it works, and who it suits**. In the next chapter, we will explore **how to analyze the market and read price charts** the skill that turns knowledge into actionable profit.

Chapter 5

Market Analysis and Price Charts

Introduction: Turning Information Into Insight

Trading without analysis is like sailing a ship without a compass you may move, but you don't know where you're going. Market analysis is the **map and compass** of every trader. It turns raw data, numbers, and charts into **actionable insight**.

Every trader, whether beginner or professional, relies on two main types of analysis:

1. **Fundamental Analysis** – understanding the intrinsic value of an asset
2. **Technical Analysis** – reading price charts to predict future movement

This chapter will guide you through both, helping you **read the market like a pro**, understand price action, and make informed decisions.

5.1 Why Market Analysis Matters

Markets are influenced by millions of factors:

- Company performance
- Economic policies
- Global events
- Investor sentiment

Without analysis, traders rely on luck. And luck is **unreliable.**

Good analysis gives you:

- Clarity in decision-making
- Confidence in entry and exit points
- A way to manage risk
- A consistent strategy for profits

"Trading is not gambling it's applied intelligence."

5.2 Fundamental Analysis: Understanding Value

Fundamental analysis is the study of **economic and financial factors** that affect an asset's value.

For Stocks

- Company earnings reports
- Revenue growth
- Profit margins
- Management decisions
- Market share and industry trends

Example:

- Company A reports 20% revenue growth and high profit margins. Its stock is likely undervalued → opportunity to buy.

For Forex

- Interest rates
- Inflation
- GDP growth
- Trade balances

Example:

- India raises interest rates → INR strengthens → forex traders adjust positions.

For Commodities

- Supply and demand
- Weather patterns
- Political events

Example:

- Drought reduces wheat production → prices rise → commodity traders profit.

Why It Matters

Fundamental analysis helps you understand **long-term trends** and decide whether an asset is **truly strong or weak.**

"Fundamentals are the heartbeat of the market. Ignore them at your own risk."

5.3 Technical Analysis: Reading the Market's Mood

While fundamental analysis focuses on value, **technical analysis (TA)** focuses on **price and volume.** It answers questions like:

- Where will the price likely go next?
- When should I enter or exit?

TA is based on the principle:

"History repeats itself."

Traders believe that **past price movements and patterns** can predict future behavior.

5.4 Charts: The Trader's Window

Price charts are **visual representations of market activity**. They are the primary tool for technical analysis.

Types of Charts

1. **Line Chart:** Simplest form; connects closing prices with a line
2. **Bar Chart:** Shows opening, closing, high, and low prices
3. **Candlestick Chart:** Most popular; displays open, high, low, and close with colored candles

Candlestick charts are like a story of the market:

- Green (or white) candles = bullish (price rose)
- Red (or black) candles = bearish (price fell)

"Charts are the heartbeat of the market read them well, and they speak volumes."

5.5 Timeframes: Seeing the Market in Layers

Different trading types use different **timeframes**:

- **Scalpers:** 1-minute to 5-minute charts
- **Intraday**: 5-minute to 1-hour charts
- **Swing**: 1-hour to daily charts
- **Positional**: Daily, weekly, or monthly charts

Timeframes are like lenses the shorter the lens, the more detailed the movement; the longer the lens, the broader the trend.

Key Takeaway

- Shorter timeframes = more noise, faster trades
- Longer timeframes = slower, more reliable trends

5.6 Trend Analysis: Following the Flow

Markets move in **trends**: upward, downward, or sideways.
Recognizing trends is crucial to profit.

- **Uptrend:** Higher highs, higher lows → buy opportunities
- **Downtrend:** Lower highs, lower lows → sell or short opportunities
- **Sideways trend:** Price moves within a range → avoid large positions, trade small

Trendlines

Drawing a straight line connecting highs or lows helps identify trends visually.

- **Support line:** Price floor where buyers appear
- **Resistance line:** Price ceiling where sellers appear

"The trend is your friend fight it, and you lose."

5.7 Support and Resistance: Market Barriers

Support and resistance are **price levels where markets reverse or stall.**

- **Support:** Price tends to stop falling
- **Resistance:** Price tends to stop rising

Example:

- Stock XYZ repeatedly falls to ₹500 but never below → ₹500 is support
- Stock rises to ₹550 repeatedly but cannot cross → ₹550 is resistance

Trading between these levels is a common strategy for beginners.

5.8 Volume Analysis: Strength Behind the Move

Volume shows **how many shares/contracts traded.**

- High volume → strong interest, trend likely to continue
- Low volume → weak interest, trend may reverse

Volume confirms price movement:

- Price rises + high volume = strong trend
- Price rises + low volume = weak trend

"Volume is the voice of the market listen closely."

5.9 Patterns: Reading Market Psychology

Price often forms **patterns**, reflecting the collective psychology of traders.

Common Patterns

1. **Head and Shoulders:** Trend reversal indicator
2. **Double Top / Bottom:** Price tested twice → reversal likely
3. **Triangles:** Continuation patterns showing consolidation
4. **Flags & Pennants:** Short-term continuation after a sharp move

Patterns give **entry and exit clues**, but always combine them with other indicators.

5.10 Indicators: Tools for Precision

Indicators are **mathematical calculations** based on price and volume. Popular ones include:

- **Moving Averages (MA):** Shows trend direction
- **Relative Strength Index (RSI):** Measures overbought or oversold conditions
- **MACD:** Trend-following momentum indicator
- **Bollinger Bands:** Price volatility and breakout points

"Indicators don't predict the future they reveal the market's behavior."

5.11 Combining Tools: The Complete Analysis

Successful traders **combine multiple tools**:

- Trendlines + Candlestick patterns + RSI
- Volume analysis + Moving averages
- Fundamental triggers + Technical confirmation

This reduces risk and increases confidence.

5.12 Risk Management Through Analysis

Analysis isn't just about profit it's about **protecting capital.**

- Set **stop-loss** levels based on support/resistance
- Avoid trades during unclear trends
- Manage position size according to risk tolerance

"The first rule of trading: don't lose money. The second rule: don't forget rule one."

5.13 Paper Trading: Practicing Without Risk

Before using real money:

- Open a **demo account**

- Practice analysis and chart reading
- Track trades, mistakes, and learning

Paper trading builds skill and confidence without financial risk.

5.14 Trading Psychology and Analysis

Even the best analysis fails without **psychological discipline**.

- Follow the plan, not emotion
- Avoid impulsive decisions
- Respect stop-loss levels

Technical tools are guides your mind executes the trade.

5.15 Summary: Mastering Market Analysis

Market analysis and price charts are your **eyes into the market**.
You've learned:

- Fundamental analysis: understanding value
- Technical analysis: reading charts, trends, and patterns
- Indicators, volume, and risk management
- The importance of practice and psychology

"Trading without analysis is guessing; analysis without discipline is meaningless. Combine both, and you see the path to consistent profit."

Chapter 6

Building Your Trading Strategy

Introduction: Turning Analysis Into Action

Knowing the market is one thing **profiting from it is another**. A trading strategy bridges the gap between **knowledge and action.**

Without a strategy, even the best analysis becomes guesswork. With one, every trade has a purpose, every decision is backed by logic, and every loss becomes a lesson.

This chapter will guide you step by step on **how to build a trading strategy** that matches your style, risk tolerance, and goals.

6.1 What is a Trading Strategy?

A trading strategy is a **plan for making decisions in the market**. It tells you:

- When to enter a trade
- When to exit a trade
- How much risk to take
- Which instruments and timeframes to use

"A strategy is not about predicting the market. It's about controlling yourself."

6.2 Why You Need a Strategy

Without a strategy:

- Emotions dictate decisions
- Impulsive trades lead to losses
- There is no method to learn from mistakes

With a strategy:

- You trade with clarity
- You can measure performance
- You can adapt and improve over time

"The market rewards preparation, not guesswork."

6.3 Components of a Trading Strategy

A complete strategy includes **five key components**:

1. **Market Selection** – Which instruments will you trade?
    - Stocks, forex, commodities, crypto, or derivatives
    - Choose based on knowledge, capital, and style
2. **Timeframe** – How long will you hold trades?
    - Scalping, intraday, swing, positional
    - Align timeframe with your lifestyle and risk tolerance
3. **Entry Criteria** – When will you enter a trade?
    - Based on technical indicators, patterns, or fundamentals
    - Example: Buy when RSI < 30 and price touches support
4. **Exit Criteria** – When will you exit a trade?
    - Take-profit levels
    - Stop-loss to limit losses
    - Trailing stops for maximizing trends
5. **Risk Management** – How much are you willing to lose per trade?
    - Usually 1–3% of your capital per trade
    - Position sizing and diversification reduce risk

6.4 Risk-Reward Ratio

Every trade should have a **risk-reward ratio**, the ratio of potential profit to potential loss.

Example:

- Buy a stock at ₹500
- Stop-loss at ₹490 → risk = ₹10
- Target = ₹530 → reward = ₹30
- Risk-reward ratio = 1:3

"A good trader loses small and lets winners grow."

A ratio above 1:2 is generally considered safe and profitable over the long term.

6.5 Position Sizing

Position sizing determines **how much of your capital you risk per trade.**

- Formula: Risk per trade ÷ (Entry price – Stop-loss)
- Example: Capital ₹100,000, risk 2% → ₹2,000 risk
- Stop-loss = ₹10 → buy 200 shares

Position sizing ensures **no single trade can wipe out your account.**

6.6 Entry Strategies

1. Breakout Trading

- Buy when price breaks above resistance
- Sell when price breaks below support

2. Pullback Trading

- Enter during a temporary retracement in the trend
- Example: In an uptrend, wait for a short dip before buying

3. Momentum Trading

- Follow strong trending moves
- Use indicators like MACD or RSI to confirm

"Your entry is the handshake with the market make it firm, precise, and confident."

6.7 Exit Strategies

Exiting is as important as entering.

- **Stop-loss:** Protects capital
- **Take-profit:** Locks in gains
- **Trailing stop:** Follows the trend, maximizing profit while limiting loss

Example:

- Buy at ₹500, target ₹550
- Place trailing stop at ₹520
- If price rises to ₹560, stop moves to ₹530
- Locks in profit automatically

"Good traders cut losses quickly and let profits run."

6.8 Combining Technical and Fundamental Analysis

Even in a single strategy, combining analysis improves accuracy.

- **Technical:** Entry and exit points
- **Fundamental:** Confirms strength of the asset

Example:

- Technical breakout in a stock
- Fundamental report shows strong earnings → higher probability of success

"Technical analysis shows where to act; fundamentals show whether to trust the signal."

6.9 Testing Your Strategy

Before using real money:

- Backtest on historical data
- Paper trade in demo accounts
- Track performance metrics: win rate, average profit, risk-reward

Testing builds **confidence and reliability**.

6.10 Adjusting and Evolving Your Strategy

Markets change, and so should your strategy:

- Adapt to volatility
- Adjust indicators
- Refine stop-loss and take-profit
- Learn from past trades

"A rigid strategy in a dynamic market is a path to failure. Flexibility is the trader's ally."

6.11 Keeping a Trading Journal

Document every trade:

- Entry and exit points
- Instruments and timeframe
- Reason for trade
- Result and lesson learned

A journal helps identify strengths, weaknesses, and patterns in your trading behavior.

6.12 Emotional Discipline

Even with a perfect strategy, emotions can ruin results:

- Fear → premature exits
- Greed → overtrading
- Impatience → skipping rules

A strategy is effective **only when followed consistently**, not adjusted impulsively.

"Discipline transforms a strategy from theory into profit."

6.13 Combining Multiple Strategies

Experienced traders often combine strategies:

- Scalping for short-term profit
- Swing trading for mid-term growth
- Positional trades for long-term wealth

But focus first on **mastering one strategy** before expanding.

6.14 Strategy for Different Market Conditions

- **Trending market:** Trend-following strategies work best
- **Sideways market:** Range-bound strategies work better

- **Volatile market:** Use tight stop-loss and smaller position sizes

"A good strategy adapts; a bad strategy stubbornly fails."

6.15 Key Principles of a Winning Strategy

1. Simplicity don't overcomplicate
2. Consistency follow rules without exception
3. Risk control never risk too much
4. Adaptability evolve with market conditions
5. Record-keeping learn from every trade

6.16 Summary: Your Roadmap to Trading Success

Building a trading strategy is **the foundation of profitable trading.** You now know:

- How to define entry and exit rules
- How to manage risk and position size
- The importance of combining analysis
- How to test, document, and refine your plan

"Strategy turns chaos into opportunity, guesswork into confidence, and knowledge into profit."

Chapter 7

Trading Psychology and Mindset

Introduction: The Mind is the Market

Trading isn't just about charts, strategies, or instruments it's **about controlling yourself**. The most successful traders aren't always the most technically skilled; they are the ones who **master their emotions.**

The market doesn't care about your feelings. Fear, greed, impatience, or overconfidence can destroy even the best strategy. This chapter dives deep into **trading psychology**, helping you cultivate the mindset needed for consistent success.

7.1 Why Psychology Matters in Trading

Even a perfect strategy can fail if your mind is not disciplined:

- **Fear** → closing trades too early
- **Greed** → overtrading or increasing risk
- **Impatience** → skipping analysis
- **Overconfidence** → ignoring signals and rules

"The market rewards skill and discipline more than emotion."

Your mind is your **most important trading tool** without mental control, all other tools are useless.

7.2 Understanding Fear in Trading

Fear is the **number one enemy of traders.** It manifests as:

- Fear of loss → hesitating to enter a trade
- Fear of missing out (FOMO) → jumping into trades without analysis
- Fear of market volatility → overreacting to price swings

How to Overcome Fear

1. Stick to your strategy
2. Use stop-loss to limit risk

3. Start with small positions
4. Practice on demo accounts

"Fear doesn't vanish; it is managed with preparation and discipline."

7.3 Greed and Overconfidence

Greed is when you try to **chase every profit opportunity**, often ignoring risk. Overconfidence comes when you **believe you can never be wrong**.

Both lead to:

- Overtrading
- Ignoring stop-loss rules
- Emotional decision-making

Managing Greed

- Set realistic profit targets
- Follow risk-reward ratios
- Celebrate consistency, not large wins

"Greed is a fast route to loss; patience is the path to wealth."

7.4 Patience: Waiting for the Right Opportunity

Patience is the foundation of trading success:

- Waiting for the **perfect setup**
- Not forcing trades during uncertain markets
- Allowing trends to develop fully

Example:

- A swing trader waits for a pullback before entering, instead of chasing the peak.

"In trading, the best trades are often the ones you don't take immediately."

7.5 Discipline: Following the Rules

Discipline means **sticking to your strategy** regardless of emotions. It's the bridge between knowledge and profit.

- Always follow entry and exit rules
- Respect stop-loss levels
- Avoid impulsive trades
- Stick to position sizing

"Discipline turns potential into performance."

7.6 Managing Stress and Emotional Balance

Trading can be stressful:

- Losing streaks may shake confidence
- Market volatility can create tension
- Watching screens constantly may lead to fatigue

Techniques for Emotional Balance

- Take breaks and step away from the screen
- Maintain a healthy lifestyle (sleep, diet, exercise)
- Use meditation or mindfulness techniques
- Focus on process, not just profits

"A calm mind makes better decisions than a stressed mind."

7.7 Controlling Impulses and FOMO

FOMO (Fear of Missing Out) drives **bad trades**. It happens when you see a sudden price spike and feel compelled to jump in.

How to Control FOMO

- Stick to your watchlist
- Only trade setups that meet your criteria
- Avoid checking prices constantly
- Accept that you will miss some moves and that's okay

"Missing a trade is better than losing capital chasing it."

7.8 Confidence Without Arrogance

Confidence is essential, but overconfidence is dangerous. True confidence comes from:

- Following your tested strategy
- Learning from past trades
- Understanding risk management

Signs of Overconfidence

- Ignoring signals
- Increasing risk impulsively
- Believing the market will always go your way

"Confidence is calm; arrogance is loud. Trade with the former."

7.9 Developing a Trader's Mindset

A strong trader mindset includes:

1. **Resilience:** Accept losses as part of learning
2. **Patience:** Wait for the right opportunities
3. **Discipline:** Follow strategy and risk rules
4. **Adaptability:** Adjust to changing market conditions
5. **Focus:** Concentrate on process, not just profits

"A trader's mind is like steel flexible yet unbreakable."

7.10 Journaling Emotions

Keeping a trading journal isn't just about numbers. Include **emotional notes**:

- How did you feel entering and exiting trades?
- Did fear or greed influence decisions?
- How did you react to losses or wins?

Analyzing emotional patterns helps **improve self-control** over time.

7.11 Learning From Losses

Losses are inevitable. Every trader experiences them. The key is to **learn, not panic.**

- Analyze what went wrong
- Identify if rules were broken
- Adjust strategy if needed
- Keep a positive mindset

"Losses are lessons in disguise. The smart trader learns; the emotional trader repeats."

7.12 Avoiding Revenge Trading

After a loss, some traders attempt to **recover immediately** by taking impulsive trades. This is called **revenge trading.**

- It usually leads to bigger losses
- Always take a step back after losing trades
- Return to the market only when calm

"Revenge belongs in life stories, not in trading accounts."

7.13 Mindset for Long-Term Success

Trading is a **marathon, not a sprint.** Focus on:

- Consistency over big wins
- Process over profits
- Learning and adaptation over chasing trends

"Wealth is built with patience, discipline, and focus — not by chasing luck."

7.14 Meditation and Mental Strength

Many top traders use **mindfulness and meditation** to improve focus and reduce stress.

Benefits include:

- Better decision-making
- Emotional control
- Reduced impulsiveness

- Improved resilience

"A calm mind sees opportunities others miss."

7.15 Key Takeaways: Master Your Mind

1. Emotions are part of trading manage them
2. Fear and greed are your biggest enemies
3. Patience and discipline are your allies
4. Confidence comes from preparation, not luck
5. Journal, review, and learn continuously

"Trading success is 80% mindset, 20% skill but without the 80%, the 20% counts for nothing."

7.16 Summary: The Trader Within

No strategy, instrument, or analysis tool can succeed without **mental mastery**.

- Trading psychology separates **profitable traders from gamblers**
- Controlling emotion ensures strategy execution
- A strong mindset is your **long-term competitive edge**

The next chapter will guide you into **practical trading setups, examples, and real market applications**, building on psychology, strategy, and analysis.

Chapter 8

Practical Trading Setups and Examples

Introduction: From Theory to Practice

By now, you've learned about **trading instruments, market analysis, strategies, and psychology**. Knowledge alone isn't enough **applying it in real market scenarios** is what separates successful traders from beginners.

This chapter will guide you through **practical trading setups**, with step-by-step examples for stocks, forex, commodities, and crypto. By the end, you'll understand **how to spot trades, execute them, and manage risk** in real situations.

8.1 Setting Up Your Trading Workspace

Before entering trades, ensure you have a **professional trading setup**:

1. **Trading Platform:** Choose one with real-time charts, news, and indicators
2. **Monitor Setup:** At least one full-screen chart; multiple screens are better
3. **Notebook/Journal:** Record every trade and thought
4. **News Feed:** Follow financial news and updates
5. **Calculator & Tools:** For position sizing, risk-reward, and stop-loss

"A prepared workspace is the foundation of a disciplined trader."

8.2 Step 1: Choosing the Instrument

Select the instrument based on:

- Your knowledge
- Risk tolerance
- Timeframe

Example:

- Beginner: Blue-chip stocks or ETFs

- Intermediate: Forex pairs or commodities
- Advanced: Crypto or derivatives

"Trade what you understand, not what's trending."

8.3 Step 2: Identifying Market Conditions

Check the **trend** and **volatility**:

- Uptrend → favor buy trades
- Downtrend → favor sell/short trades
- Sideways → range trading or wait

Use charts and indicators to **confirm trends.**

8.4 Step 3: Choosing a Setup Type

Popular Trading Setups

1. **Breakout Setup**
    - Price breaks key support/resistance
    - Confirm with volume spike

Example:

- Stock XYZ resistance at ₹500
- Price breaks ₹500 with high volume → enter long
- Stop-loss: ₹490, Target: ₹530

1. **Pullback Setup**
    - Price retraces temporarily in a trend
    - Enter near support in an uptrend or resistance in a downtrend

Example:

- Uptrend in EUR/USD
- Price dips to 1.1800 (support) → buy
- Stop-loss: 1.1780, Target: 1.1850

1. **Momentum Setup**
   - Enter strong trending moves confirmed by indicators
   - MACD crossover, RSI above 50, or moving average breakout

Example:

- BTC price surges past 50-day MA
- RSI confirms strength → enter long
- Stop-loss at previous swing low

8.5 Step 4: Defining Entry and Exit

Every trade must have clear rules:

- **Entry Point:** Based on setup confirmation
- **Stop-Loss:** Limit potential loss
- **Take-Profit:** Lock in gains

Example for a stock trade:

- Entry: ₹500 (breakout)
- Stop-loss: ₹490 (support)
- Target: ₹530 (resistance)

"Plan your trade and trade your plan."

8.6 Step 5: Calculating Risk and Position Size

Always know how much capital is at risk:

- Capital: ₹100,000
- Risk per trade: 2% → ₹2,000
- Stop-loss distance: ₹10 → Buy 200 shares

This ensures **a single loss cannot destroy your account.**

8.7 Step 6: Monitoring the Trade

Once in the trade:

- Watch price action, volume, and news
- Adjust stop-loss if trend strengthens (trailing stop)
- Stick to exit rules; avoid emotional decisions

"The market moves; your strategy guides your reaction."

8.8 Example 1: Stock Breakout Trade

- **Stock:** ABC Ltd
- **Trend:** Uptrend
- **Setup:** Breakout of ₹200 resistance
- **Volume:** High
- **Entry:** ₹201
- **Stop-loss:** ₹195
- **Target:** ₹220

Trade Result:

- Price reaches ₹220 → Profit ₹19 per share
- Risk-reward ratio: 1:3
- Lesson: Follow setup, use stop-loss, and let profits run

8.9 Example 2: Forex Pullback Trade

- **Pair:** EUR/USD
- **Trend:** Uptrend
- **Setup:** Pullback to support 1.1800
- **Entry:** 1.1810
- **Stop-loss:** 1.1780
- **Target:** 1.1850

Trade Result:

- Price rises to 1.1850 → Profit 40 pips
- Lesson: Patience during pullbacks pays

8.10 Example 3: Commodity Momentum Trade

- **Commodity:** Gold
- **Trend:** Strong upward breakout
- **Indicators:** MACD crossover, RSI 60
- **Entry:** $2,000 per ounce
- **Stop-loss:** $1,980
- **Target:** $2,050

Trade Result:

- Price hits target → Profit $50 per ounce
- Lesson: Momentum trading works with strong trends

8.11 Example 4: Crypto Range Trade

- **Asset:** Bitcoin
- **Trend:** Sideways
- **Setup:** Range-bound between $28,000–$30,000
- **Entry:** $28,200 (buy near support)
- **Stop-loss:** $27,800
- **Target:** $29,800

Trade Result:

- Price moves within range → Profit $1,600
- Lesson: Even sideways markets provide opportunities

8.12 Using Stop-Loss and Take-Profit Orders

Automated orders reduce emotional decisions:

- **Stop-Loss:** Exit if trade goes wrong

- **Take-Profit:** Exit when target achieved
- **Trailing Stop:** Adjust as trend moves favorably

"Stops are not a restriction; they are protection."

8.13 Combining Multiple Trades

- Diversify across instruments and setups
- Don't put all capital into one trade
- Balance risk and reward across portfolio

"A single trade doesn't define you consistent execution does."

8.14 Journaling and Review

After every trade, record:

- Setup type
- Entry/exit points
- Risk/reward
- Result
- Lessons learned

Review weekly to **identify strengths and weaknesses.**

8.15 Common Mistakes in Practical Trading

- Ignoring stop-loss
- Overleveraging
- Entering trades without confirmation
- Chasing every move
- Ignoring market conditions

Avoid these to **protect capital and build consistency**.

8.16 Key Takeaways: Practical Trading in Action

1. Prepare workspace and platform
2. Choose instruments and market conditions wisely
3. Identify setup type and follow entry/exit rules

4. Calculate risk and manage position size
5. Monitor trades and stick to strategy
6. Review and learn from every trade

"Theory teaches you the game; practice teaches you to win it."

Chapter 9

Risk Management and Capital Protection

Introduction: Protecting Your Most Important Asset

In trading, the first rule is simple: **don't lose money**. While profits excite, losses can destroy accounts and confidence. Risk management is **the backbone of successful trading**, ensuring that your capital survives even during tough market conditions.

This chapter will teach you how to **manage risk, protect capital, and trade sustainably** — the difference between short-term excitement and long-term wealth.

9.1 Why Risk Management Matters

Markets are unpredictable:

- No strategy guarantees profit
- Even experienced traders face losses
- Emotional decisions increase risk

By managing risk:

- You survive losing streaks
- You protect your capital for future opportunities
- You can trade confidently and consistently

"Preserve your capital first; profits will follow."

9.2 The Concept of Risk in Trading

Risk is the **possibility of losing money** on a trade.
Every trade has two sides:

1. **Potential profit** – why you enter
2. **Potential loss** – what you must be ready to accept

Example:

- Buy a stock at ₹500
- Stop-loss at ₹490 → risk ₹10 per share
- Target ₹530 → reward ₹30 per share

Risk is **controllable**, while profit is **uncertain**. Smart traders focus on what they can control.

9.3 Position Sizing: Controlling Exposure

Position sizing determines **how much of your capital is at risk per trade.**

Steps to Calculate Position Size

1. Decide total capital: ₹100,000
2. Decide risk per trade: 2% → ₹2,000
3. Identify stop-loss distance: ₹10
4. Calculate shares/contracts: ₹2,000 ÷ ₹10 = 200 shares

Key principle: Never risk more than a small percentage of your capital on a single trade.

"Small losses protect your capital; big losses can destroy it."

9.4 Stop-Loss Orders: Your Safety Net

A stop-loss is an order to **automatically exit a trade** at a predetermined price.

Benefits:

- Limits losses
- Removes emotional decisions
- Provides peace of mind

Types of Stop-Loss

1. **Fixed Stop-Loss:** Predefined price
2. **Trailing Stop:** Adjusts with price movement
3. **Volatility Stop:** Based on market volatility

"Stop-loss is not a restriction; it's protection for your future trades."

9.5 Risk-Reward Ratio

Every trade should have a **favorable risk-reward ratio.**
Example:

- Entry: ₹500
- Stop-loss: ₹490 → risk ₹10
- Target: ₹530 → reward ₹30
- Risk-reward ratio = 1:3

Aim for trades where **potential reward outweighs risk**. Even if only 50% of trades succeed, 1:3 ratio ensures long-term profitability.

9.6 Diversification: Don't Put All Eggs in One Basket

Diversification spreads risk across instruments, sectors, or markets:

- **Stocks**: Different sectors
- **Forex**: Multiple currency pairs
- **Commodities**: Metals, oil, agriculture
- **Crypto**: Bitcoin, Ethereum, and others

Diversification **reduces the impact of a single loss** and smooths overall returns.

9.7 Hedging: Reducing Risk Exposure

Hedging involves taking **opposite positions** to protect against losses:

- Buy an asset → hedge with options or futures
- Forex traders use correlated pairs
- Commodity traders hedge with derivatives

"Hedging is like insurance for your trades."

9.8 Understanding Volatility Risk

Volatility is **price fluctuation over time**. High volatility can bring high profits but also high losses.

Strategies to manage volatility:

- Reduce position size in volatile markets
- Use tighter stop-losses
- Avoid overleveraging

"Volatility is a double-edged sword respect it."

9.9 Capital Allocation

Your total trading capital should be **allocated wisely**:

- 60% for safe, steady trades
- 30% for moderate-risk setups
- 10% for high-risk, high-reward opportunities

Never risk more than **a portion of your total capital** on a single trade.
"Your capital is the fuel; manage it wisely or the journey ends prematurely."

9.10 Emotional Risk Management

Even the best strategies fail without emotional control:

- Avoid revenge trading after a loss
- Don't increase risk impulsively
- Stick to position sizing and stop-loss rules

"Emotions can destroy discipline faster than the market can."

9.11 Common Risk Management Mistakes

1. Ignoring stop-loss
2. Overleveraging
3. Chasing every trade
4. Trading with too much capital on one instrument
5. Ignoring market conditions

Avoid these mistakes to **protect capital and build consistency**.

9.12 Risk Management Tools

Modern trading platforms offer tools to **control risk automatically**:

- Stop-loss and take-profit orders

- Trailing stops
- Alerts and notifications
- Position sizing calculators

Using these tools increases efficiency and reduces emotional trading.

9.13 Review and Adjust

Regularly review your trades:

- Which trades followed risk rules?
- Were losses within acceptable limits?
- How did emotional decisions impact results?

Adjust strategies and position sizes based on **experience and market conditions.**

9.14 Key Principles of Capital Protection

1. Risk only a small portion of your capital per trade
2. Use stop-losses consistently
3. Diversify across instruments and sectors
4. Avoid emotional trading
5. Always plan for losses before targeting profits

"Preserve capital like a treasure it is the foundation of future profits."

9.15 Summary: The Safety Net of Successful Trading

Risk management ensures that **no single loss ends your trading journey**.

- Position sizing, stop-loss, and risk-reward ratio protect your account
- Diversification and hedging reduce exposure
- Emotional discipline strengthens decision-making

"In trading, survival is the first rule. Everything else profits, growth, success comes after."

The next chapter will focus on **trading tools, platforms, and technology**, showing how to implement strategies and manage risk effectively in the modern trading environment.

Chapter 10

Trading Tools,Platforms, and Technology

Introduction: Equip Yourself for Success

Trading today is **not just about knowledge or intuition** it's also about using the right tools and technology. A modern trader relies on platforms, charts, indicators, and software to **analyze markets, execute trades, and manage risk efficiently**.

This chapter will guide you through the essential tools, trading platforms, and technology you need to **trade effectively in any market**.

10.1 Why Tools and Technology Matter

Imagine trying to navigate a ship without instruments. That's what trading without tools is like:

- Charts help identify trends
- Indicators improve timing
- Platforms provide speed and accuracy
- Alerts prevent missed opportunities

"Knowledge is power, but the right tools turn power into results."

10.2 Trading Platforms: Your Digital Workspace

A trading platform is where all the action happens. It's your **digital command center**.

Popular Features

1. Real-time charts
2. Order execution (buy/sell)
3. Technical indicators
4. Alerts and notifications
5. Risk management tools
6. News feeds and market data

Popular Platforms

- **Stocks:** Zerodha, Upstox, TD Ameritrade, Interactive Brokers
- **Forex:** MetaTrader 4/5, cTrader
- **Crypto:** Binance, Coinbase, Kraken
- **Commodities:** MCX, TradingView, NinjaTrader

"Choose a platform that suits your trading style, reliability, and ease of use."

10.3 Charting Tools: Reading Market Movements

Charts visualize **price action and trends.** Effective charting tools allow you to:

- Zoom in/out on timeframes
- Apply technical indicators
- Draw trendlines, support/resistance, and channels
- Compare multiple instruments

Example: TradingView offers advanced charting, real-time data, and social community ideas.

"Charts are your eyes into the market; make them sharp and clear."

10.4 Technical Indicators and Analysis Tools

Indicators are mathematical calculations based on **price and volume.** They help predict trends, momentum, and reversals.

Essential Indicators

1. **Moving Averages (MA):** Trend direction
2. **Relative Strength Index (RSI):** Overbought/oversold
3. **MACD:** Momentum and trend changes
4. **Bollinger Bands:** Volatility and potential breakouts
5. **Fibonacci Retracements:** Support/resistance levels

"Indicators guide your decisions; they don't replace your judgment."

10.5 Order Types and Execution Tools

Trading platforms offer various **order types** to control trades:

1. **Market Order:** Buy/sell at the current price

2. **Limit Order:** Buy/sell at a specific price
3. **Stop-Loss Order:** Exit automatically if price moves against you
4. **Trailing Stop:** Adjusts with market movement to lock profits
5. **OCO (One Cancels Other):** Combine stop-loss and take-profit

"Order types are the safety mechanisms that protect capital and profits."

10.6 Automated Trading and Bots

Technology allows automation:

- **Expert Advisors (EA) or Trading Bots** execute trades automatically
- Follow predefined rules for entry, exit, and risk management
- Useful for high-frequency or repetitive strategies

Benefits:

- Remove emotions from trading
- Execute faster than humans
- Monitor multiple markets simultaneously

"Automation is not cheating; it's efficiency with discipline."

10.7 News Feeds and Market Alerts

Markets respond to news instantly. Timely information can **make or break trades**:

- Economic releases (GDP, inflation, interest rates)
- Corporate announcements and earnings reports
- Political and global events

Platforms often provide **alerts and notifications** for price levels, trends, or news, ensuring you **never miss an opportunity**.

10.8 Risk Management Tools

Technology supports **risk management**:

- Stop-loss and take-profit automation
- Position sizing calculators

- Portfolio monitoring dashboards
- Volatility alerts

"The smarter the tool, the safer your trades."

10.9 Backtesting and Strategy Development Software

Before committing real money, test your strategies using historical data:

- Check past performance of setups
- Optimize indicators and entry/exit rules
- Platforms like TradingView, NinjaTrader, and MetaTrader allow backtesting

"Backtesting is rehearsal; practice makes perfect before the show."

10.10 Mobile Trading Apps

Modern traders need **mobility**:

- Monitor trades anytime, anywhere
- Quick execution during market movements
- Notifications for setups, news, and alerts

Popular mobile apps: Zerodha Kite, Upstox Pro, Binance App, MetaTrader Mobile

"A trader's eyes and hands must move with the market, not lag behind."

10.11 Integrating Tools for Maximum Efficiency

Successful traders combine multiple tools:

1. **Platform + Charting** for market analysis
2. **Indicators + Alerts** for confirmation
3. **Mobile + Desktop** for flexibility
4. **Automation + Backtesting** for consistency

"The right combination of tools turns preparation into performance."

10.12 Technology Tips for Beginners

- Start simple, don't overload with tools
- Learn each platform feature gradually
- Use demo accounts before real money
- Keep software updated
- Protect accounts with passwords and two-factor authentication

"Technology is powerful, but only if you control it."

10.13 Common Mistakes in Using Trading Technology

1. Over-relying on indicators
2. Ignoring fundamentals
3. Chasing alerts without strategy
4. Neglecting risk management
5. Jumping into automated systems blindly

Avoid these mistakes to **maximize the advantage of technology**.

10.14 Summary: Equip Yourself for Modern Trading

Trading tools, platforms, and technology **amplify your skills**:

- Platforms are your command center
- Charts and indicators guide decisions
- Orders and automation protect capital and profits
- News, alerts, and mobile apps keep you updated

"Technology is the extension of a trader's mind use it wisely to make smarter, faster, and safer decisions."

The next chapter will focus on **different trading styles, choosing what suits you best, and aligning your strategy with your lifestyle and goals**

Chapter 11

Trading Styles & Choosing What Suits You

Introduction: Trading Your Way

Trading is not one-size-fits-all. Each trader has a unique **personality, lifestyle, capital, and risk tolerance**, which influences the style of trading that fits best. Choosing the right style is crucial it affects your **profitability, stress levels, and consistency**.

This chapter explores **popular trading styles**, their advantages, challenges, and how to select the one that aligns with your goals.

11.1 Why Trading Style Matters

Your trading style determines:

- Time spent analyzing markets
- Frequency of trades
- Risk exposure per trade
- Type of instruments traded

Choosing the wrong style can lead to **frustration, stress, and losses**. The right style allows you to trade **comfortably, consistently, and confidently**.

"Success in trading comes from matching strategy to personality, not forcing yourself into someone else's mold."

11.2 Scalping: Quick Moves, Quick Profits

What is Scalping?

- Short-term trading style
- Trades last from **seconds to minutes**
- Focus on small price movements

Who is it for?

- Traders who can focus intensely
- Quick decision-makers
- Comfortable with high-frequency trading

Advantages

- Many opportunities per day
- Small, frequent profits
- Less exposure to overnight risk

Challenges

- Requires constant attention
- High transaction costs
- Can be stressful

"Scalping is like sprinting fast, precise, and demanding."

11.3 Day Trading: Profiting Within the Day

What is Day Trading?

- Enter and exit trades **within the same day**
- Avoids overnight risk
- Uses charts, indicators, and news

Who is it for?

- Traders with a few hours per day to focus
- Comfortable with moderate risk
- Able to make decisions under pressure

Advantages

- No overnight exposure
- Multiple setups per day
- Flexibility in markets and instruments

Challenges

- Requires focus and discipline
- Can be emotionally demanding
- Learning curve for timing and analysis

"Day trading is like playing chess in real time strategy, patience, and quick thinking."

11.4 Swing Trading: Riding the Trends

What is Swing Trading?

- Trades last **days to weeks**
- Capitalizes on trends and price swings
- Uses technical analysis primarily

Who is it for?

- Traders with limited daily screen time
- Comfortable holding trades overnight
- Patient, strategic thinkers

Advantages

- Less stressful than day trading
- Larger potential gains per trade
- Easier to balance with a lifestyle

Challenges

- Overnight market risk
- Requires trend analysis and patience
- Fewer trades compared to day trading

"Swing trading is like surfing catching the wave and riding it with balance."

11.5 Position Trading: Long-Term Perspective

What is Position Trading?

- Trades last **weeks to months**
- Focuses on long-term trends and fundamentals
- Less reliant on short-term fluctuations

Who is it for?

- Traders who prefer slow, steady growth
- Busy professionals or part-time traders
- Comfortable with lower frequency, higher patience

Advantages

- Less screen time
- Lower stress from daily market fluctuations
- Focus on bigger profits per trade

Challenges

- Requires patience and strong capital
- Exposure to market news and events
- Slower feedback on performance

"Position trading is like planting a tree nurture it, and it grows strong over time."

11.6 Algorithmic and Automated Trading

What is Algorithmic Trading?

- Using **computer programs or bots** to execute trades
- Follows pre-set rules for entry, exit, and risk
- Can operate 24/7

Who is it for?

- Technically skilled traders
- Those who prefer automation
- High-frequency, data-driven trading

Advantages

- Eliminates emotions
- Fast execution and monitoring of multiple markets
- Consistency in strategy

Challenges

- Requires programming knowledge
- System errors or glitches can cause losses
- Strategy must be tested extensively

"Algorithmic trading is precision engineered efficiency meets strategy."

11.7 Choosing the Right Style for You

Consider these factors:

1. **Time Availability**
    - Full-time → Day or swing trading
    - Part-time → Swing or position trading
2. **Personality**
    - Fast, energetic → Scalping or day trading
    - Patient, analytical → Swing or position trading
3. **Capital**
    - Small capital → Short-term trades, focus on high probability setups
    - Large capital → Longer-term trades, diversified portfolios
4. **Risk Tolerance**
    - High → Scalping, day trading
    - Moderate → Swing trading
    - Low → Position trading

"The best trading style is the one you can follow consistently with discipline and confidence."

11.8 Combining Styles

Some traders combine styles to **maximize opportunities**:

- Swing + Position: Capture mid-term trends and long-term growth
- Day + Swing: Focus on daily trades while holding select longer-term positions

Start with one style, master it, then experiment gradually.

11.9 Testing Your Style

- Open a **demo account**
- Practice the chosen style
- Track performance, emotional comfort, and profitability
- Adjust style based on results

"Your trading style should suit you, not the market. Adaptation comes with experience."

11.10 Key Principles in Choosing Your Style

1. Align style with personality and lifestyle
2. Match style with capital and risk tolerance
3. Practice before committing real money
4. Be flexible and ready to evolve
5. Focus on consistency over chasing trends

"Trading success is not about speed or frequency it's about alignment with yourself."

11.11 Summary: Trading Your Way to Success

Choosing a trading style is about **personal alignment**:

- Scalping → Fast, short-term action
- Day trading → Active, intraday focus
- Swing trading → Patient, trend-focused
- Position trading → Long-term, fundamental-based
- Algorithmic → Automated, precise execution

Once you identify the style that fits your **time, personality, and goals**, all other trading skills strategy, psychology, and risk management become more effective.

Chapter 12

Building Your Personal Trading Plan

Introduction: Your Roadmap to Consistent Success

Trading without a plan is like navigating a ship without a compass you may move, but you won't know where you're heading. A **personal trading plan** is your roadmap: it guides decisions, manages risk, and turns knowledge into consistent profits.

This chapter will help you **create a complete trading plan** tailored to your style, goals, capital, and personality.

12.1 Why a Trading Plan is Essential

A trading plan provides:

- **Structure:** Clear rules for entry, exit, and risk
- **Consistency:** Reduces emotional trading
- **Discipline:** Keeps you focused on your strategy
- **Measurement:** Tracks performance for continuous improvement

"A plan doesn't guarantee profits, but it guarantees control."

12.2 Components of a Trading Plan

A solid plan has **seven key components**:

1. **Trading Goals** – What do you want to achieve?
2. **Trading Style** – Scalping, day, swing, position, or automated
3. **Market Selection** – Stocks, forex, commodities, crypto
4. **Strategy Rules** – Entry, exit, indicators, confirmation
5. **Risk Management** – Position size, stop-loss, risk-reward
6. **Psychology & Discipline** – Handling emotions, journaling
7. **Review & Improvement** – Tracking results and refining strategy

"Your plan is your contract with yourself follow it faithfully."

12.3 Setting Trading Goals

Goals guide your **focus and motivation**:

- Short-term: Daily, weekly, or monthly targets
- Long-term: Yearly profit, portfolio growth, or skill mastery
- Focus on **realistic and measurable goals**

Example:

- Short-term: Make 5 profitable trades per week with <2% risk per trade
- Long-term: Grow capital 20% per year consistently

"Goals give direction, not excuses."

12.4 Choosing Your Trading Style

Your plan must **align with your personality and lifestyle**:

- Full-time → Day or swing trading
- Part-time → Swing or position trading
- Personality → Fast-paced for scalping, patient for swing/position

"Your trading plan is only effective if it suits who you are."

12.5 Market and Instrument Selection

Choose markets based on:

- Knowledge and comfort
- Capital requirements
- Volatility and liquidity

Example:

- Beginners: Blue-chip stocks, major forex pairs
- Experienced: Options, commodities, crypto

"Trade what you understand, not what everyone else is trading."

12.6 Defining Strategy Rules

Every trade in your plan should have **clear rules**:

- **Entry Criteria:** Conditions for initiating a trade
- **Exit Criteria:** Stop-loss, take-profit, and trailing rules
- **Confirmation Tools:** Indicators, patterns, or news

Example:

- Buy stock when price breaks above resistance with volume spike
- Stop-loss 2% below entry
- Target 5% above entry

"Rules remove guesswork and guard your capital."

12.7 Risk Management in Your Plan

Include precise **risk management guidelines**:

- Maximum % of capital risked per trade
- Daily, weekly, or monthly loss limits
- Diversification rules
- Position sizing formulas

"Capital preservation is the foundation everything else is built on it."

12.8 Psychology and Discipline

Plan for your **emotional control**:

- Record emotional state during trades
- Avoid revenge trading after losses
- Stick to stop-loss and profit-taking rules
- Practice patience and consistency

"A trading plan without emotional rules is like a car without brakes."

12.9 Journaling and Record Keeping

Your plan must include a **trade journal**:

- Record setup type, entry, exit, profit/loss
- Note emotions, mistakes, and lessons
- Review weekly and monthly to improve

"A journal transforms experience into wisdom."

12.10 Reviewing and Improving the Plan

Markets evolve, and so should your plan:

- Review trades and performance
- Identify weaknesses or missed opportunities
- Adjust strategy, risk rules, or instruments accordingly

"Your plan is alive; it grows as you grow."

12.11 Sample Personal Trading Plan Structure

1. Goals

- Short-term: 5 profitable trades/week
- Long-term: 20% annual growth

2. Style

- Swing trading

3. Market

- Stocks, major forex pairs

4. Strategy Rules

- Breakout setups with volume confirmation
- Stop-loss 2% below entry, target 5% above

5. Risk Management

- Max 2% risk per trade
- Max 5% capital loss per week

6. Psychology

- Avoid impulsive trades

- Journal all trades and emotions

7. Review

- Weekly performance analysis
- Adjust rules based on results

"This structure keeps your trading organized, focused, and accountable."

12.12 Tips for a Practical Trading Plan

1. Start simple, avoid overcomplicating
2. Focus on one or two strategies initially
3. Use demo trading to refine the plan
4. Include realistic goals and risk limits
5. Review and update regularly

"A plan is a living document use it, test it, and improve it."

12.13 Key Takeaways: Your Personal Roadmap

- A trading plan is your **guide to consistency and discipline**
- Include goals, style, strategy, risk management, and psychology
- Record every trade and review performance regularly
- Adjust the plan based on experience and market changes

"A trader without a plan is a wanderer; a trader with a plan is a navigator."

Chapter 13

Advanced Technical Analysis Techniques

Introduction: Seeing the Market Beyond the Obvious

By now, you understand basic chart patterns, indicators, and trend analysis. Advanced technical analysis takes this **to the next level**, helping you **anticipate price movements, refine entries and exits, and gain an edge in the market.**

This chapter covers **higher-level techniques, patterns, and methods** that professional traders use to enhance decision-making.

13.1 Why Advanced Technical Analysis Matters

Markets are influenced by countless factors, from investor psychology to global events. Advanced technical analysis helps you:

- Identify stronger trends
- Spot reversals earlier
- Confirm trade setups
- Reduce false signals

"The more precise your analysis, the higher the probability of successful trades."

13.2 Candlestick Patterns: Reading Market Sentiment

Candlestick charts reveal **market psychology** in real time. Advanced traders look for patterns that indicate **trend continuation or reversal.**

Key Patterns

1. **Engulfing Pattern:** Strong reversal signal
2. **Doji:** Market indecision, potential reversal
3. **Hammer and Hanging Man:** Reversal confirmation at support/ resistance
4. **Morning and Evening Star:** Major trend reversal signals

"Candlesticks are the heartbeat of the market read it carefully."

13.3 Chart Patterns: Geometry of Price

Classic chart patterns help predict **future movements:**

1. **Head and Shoulders:** Reversal of trend
2. **Double Top/Bottom:** Trend exhaustion and reversal
3. **Triangles (Symmetrical, Ascending, Descending):** Continuation or breakout
4. **Flags and Pennants:** Short-term continuation patterns

"Patterns form because traders repeat behavior learning them is like learning human psychology."

13.4 Support and Resistance: The Invisible Walls

Support and resistance are **price levels where the market reacts repeatedly**.

- **Support:** Price floor where buying pressure emerges
- **Resistance:** Price ceiling where selling pressure emerges

Advanced Techniques

- Use multiple timeframes to confirm levels
- Look for confluence with Fibonacci retracements or moving averages
- Combine with volume to validate strength

"Support and resistance are your market guideposts never trade blindly past them."

13.5 Trendlines and Channels

Trendlines connect swing highs and lows to **visualize the market direction**:

- **Uptrend:** Higher highs and higher lows
- **Downtrend:** Lower highs and lower lows
- **Channels:** Parallel trendlines indicate consistent trend range

Advanced Applications

- Breakout from trendline = strong signal
- Test of trendline = potential entry point

- Combine with momentum indicators for confirmation

"Trendlines are the skeleton of the market understand its structure."

13.6 Fibonacci Tools

Fibonacci retracement and extension levels reveal **key support, resistance, and profit targets**:

- Common retracement levels: 23.6%, 38.2%, 50%, 61.8%
- Use to identify pullback levels in trends
- Combine with other indicators for confirmation

"Fibonacci is the secret math behind market moves it shows where price may respect natural ratios."

13.7 Moving Averages: Dynamic Support and Resistance

Moving averages smooth price data and **highlight trends**:

- **Simple Moving Average (SMA):** Average over time
- **Exponential Moving Average (EMA):** Gives more weight to recent price

Advanced Techniques

- Crossovers (EMA 50 vs 200) for trend confirmation
- Dynamic support/resistance on trending markets
- Combine with RSI or MACD for entry signals

"Moving averages are trend filters they help separate signal from noise."

13.8 Volume Analysis: Confirming Moves

Volume validates price action:

- High volume + price breakout = strong signal
- Low volume + breakout = weak, possibly false signal
- Volume spikes often precede reversals

Techniques

- On-Balance Volume (OBV)
- Volume Weighted Average Price (VWAP)
- Accumulation/Distribution analysis

"Volume is the truth behind price it shows who really controls the market."

13.9 Oscillators for Momentum and Reversals

Oscillators identify overbought/oversold conditions:

- **RSI (Relative Strength Index):** 70+ = overbought, 30- = oversold
- **MACD (Moving Average Convergence Divergence):** Trend strength and reversals
- **Stochastic Oscillator:** Momentum and potential reversal signals

"Oscillators give early warnings but always confirm with price action."

13.10 Multiple Timeframe Analysis

Analyze the same instrument on different timeframes:

- **Higher timeframe:** Defines overall trend
- **Lower timeframe:** Identifies precise entry and exit
- Example: Weekly trend + daily setup + hourly entry

"Timeframes are layers of clarity zoom in and out to see the full picture."

13.11 Confluence: Combining Tools for Higher Probability

Confluence is when multiple signals align:

- Trendline + Fibonacci level + candlestick pattern + volume spike
- Increases confidence and probability of success

"One tool gives a hint; multiple aligned tools give conviction."

13.12 Advanced Pattern Trading Examples

1. **Breakout Trade Example**

- Stock breaks triangle resistance
- Volume spike confirms
- RSI not overbought
- Entry, stop-loss, target calculated

2. **Reversal Trade Example**
    - Double bottom forms at support
    - Hammer candlestick confirms reversal
    - MACD bullish crossover
    - Entry at confirmation candle

"Advanced analysis is about seeing what others miss the hidden signals."

13.13 Common Mistakes in Advanced Analysis

- Overloading charts with too many indicators
- Ignoring volume and context
- Trading patterns without confirmation
- Neglecting risk management

"Advanced tools are powerful but discipline and simplicity win in the long run."

13.14 Key Takeaways: Mastering Technical Analysis

1. Learn to read candlesticks and chart patterns
2. Use support, resistance, trendlines, and channels wisely
3. Combine Fibonacci, moving averages, and volume for precision
4. Use oscillators for momentum and reversal insights
5. Seek confluence for high-probability trades
6. Always validate with risk management

"Advanced technical analysis is not magic it's structured observation, pattern recognition, and probability."

13.15 Summary: Seeing the Market Clearly

Advanced technical analysis gives traders **clarity and confidence**. By combining price action, patterns, volume, and indicators, you can:

- Anticipate market movements
- Refine entries and exits
- Increase probability of profitable trades

The next chapter will focus on **trading strategies in different markets**, showing how to apply these advanced techniques in stocks, forex, commodities, and crypto.

Chapter 14

Trading Strategies for Different Markets

Introduction: Adapting Strategies to Each Market

Markets are different stocks, forex, commodities, and crypto all move with their own rhythm. A strategy that works in one may not work in another. Successful traders **adapt techniques to the specific market**, combining knowledge, tools, and risk management.

This chapter will guide you through **market-specific strategies**, helping you trade effectively in any environment.

14.1 Stock Market Strategies

Stocks are influenced by **company fundamentals, sector trends, and market sentiment.**

Popular Stock Trading Strategies

1. **Breakout Trading**
    - Buy above resistance or sell below support
    - Confirm with volume spike
    - Works well in trending stocks
2. **Gap Trading**
    - Exploit overnight gaps in price
    - Gap up → potential continuation or reversal
    - Use stop-loss near gap edge
3. **Dividend Capture Strategy**
    - Buy before dividend ex-date
    - Hold short-term for dividend profit
4. **Swing Trading**
    - Use trend-following indicators
    - Hold for days to weeks
    - Ideal for balancing work and trading

"Stocks reward patience and trend recognition don't chase them blindly."

14.2 Forex Trading Strategies

Forex markets are highly liquid and sensitive to **global economic events.**
Popular Forex Strategies

1. **Trend Following**
    - Identify currency pair trends
    - Use moving averages and RSI
    - Enter pullbacks in the trend

1. **Carry Trade**
    - Buy high-yield currency, sell low-yield currency
    - Profits from interest rate differentials
2. **News Trading**
    - Trade major economic releases
    - Requires fast execution and discipline
3. **Range Trading**
    - Trade support/resistance in consolidating pairs
    - Use oscillators like RSI or Stochastic

"Forex rewards strategy and timing knowledge of global events is crucial."

14.3 Commodity Trading Strategies

Commodities like **gold, oil, and agricultural products** are influenced by **supply, demand, and global events.**
Popular Commodity Strategies

1. **Trend Following**
    - Use moving averages, MACD, or Bollinger Bands
    - Ride long-term trends in oil, metals, or grains
2. **Seasonal Patterns**
    - Certain commodities follow predictable cycles
    - Example: Agricultural commodities in harvest seasons
3. **Spread Trading**
    - Buy one commodity, sell another correlated commodity
    - Reduce risk while capturing relative price movements

4. **Breakout Trading**
    - Identify key support/resistance
    - Trade significant price moves with volume confirmation

"Commodity trading requires understanding fundamentals and global supply-demand factors."

14.4 Crypto Trading Strategies

Cryptocurrencies are **highly volatile** and operate 24/7, offering unique opportunities.

Popular Crypto Strategies

1. **Momentum Trading**
    - Trade strong trending coins
    - Confirm with volume and RSI
2. **Swing Trading**
    - Identify support and resistance
    - Hold for a few days or weeks
3. **Arbitrage**
    - Exploit price differences across exchanges
    - Requires speed and automation
4. **Scalping**
    - High-frequency trades capturing small price moves
    - Works best on high-liquidity coins like BTC or ETH

"Crypto trading demands discipline, patience, and quick decision-making."

14.5 Adapting Strategies Across Markets

While strategies vary, some principles **apply to all markets**:

- Trend following works in stocks, forex, commodities, and crypto
- Breakouts require volume confirmation everywhere
- Support/resistance and candlestick patterns are universal
- Risk management is essential regardless of market

"Master the principles, then adapt the techniques to each market."

14.6 Combining Markets for Diversification

Professional traders diversify across markets to **spread risk and exploit opportunities:**

- Stocks + Forex: Balance long-term growth with intraday opportunities
- Commodities + Crypto: Hedge against market volatility
- Multi-market approach ensures smoother portfolio performance

"Diversification is not just protection it's a strategy for consistent growth."

14.7 Practical Examples: Market-Specific Trades

Stock Trade Example

- Stock XYZ breaks resistance at ₹500
- Volume spike confirms
- Entry: ₹501, Stop-loss: ₹490, Target: ₹530
- Result: Trend following breakout strategy succeeds

Forex Trade Example

- EUR/USD pulls back to 1.1800 in uptrend
- RSI confirms oversold
- Entry: 1.1810, Stop-loss: 1.1780, Target: 1.1850
- Result: Swing trade captures 40 pips

Commodity Trade Example

- Gold breaks upward trendline with volume
- Entry: $2,000, Stop-loss: $1,980, Target: $2,050
- Result: Trend-following strategy profitable

Crypto Trade Example

- BTC surges past $30,000, RSI confirms momentum
- Entry: $30,100, Stop-loss: $29,500, Target: $31,500

- Result: Momentum strategy yields profit

"Apply the right strategy to the right market that's where consistent profits come from."

14.8 Common Mistakes Across Markets

- Using the same strategy everywhere without adaptation
- Ignoring market-specific factors like news, volatility, or liquidity
- Overleveraging in volatile markets
- Trading without proper risk management

"Adaptation and discipline separate successful traders from gamblers."

14.9 Key Takeaways: Strategies Across Markets

1. Choose strategies suited to each market
2. Trend following, breakouts, and pullbacks work universally
3. Understand market-specific drivers
4. Combine markets for diversification
5. Always apply risk management

"A versatile trader knows principles and adapts them to every market."

14.10 Summary: Trading Success Across Markets

Every market has unique characteristics, but **the core principles remain the same:**

- Analyze trends, patterns, and momentum
- Confirm with volume and indicators
- Apply disciplined risk management
- Choose the strategy that fits the market and your style

Chapter 15

Developing a Trading Mindset

Introduction: The Mind as Your Greatest Asset

Trading is more than charts, indicators, or strategies it is **a mental game.** Your mindset determines whether you succeed or fail. Even the best strategy can fail if the trader cannot control emotions, maintain discipline, or think clearly under pressure.

This chapter focuses on **building the mindset of a consistent and confident trader**, teaching how to handle fear, greed, and uncertainty.

15.1 Why Mindset Matters in Trading

Markets are unpredictable, and losses are inevitable. A strong mindset helps you:

- Stick to your trading plan
- Handle losses without panic
- Avoid impulsive decisions
- Maintain consistency over time

"Trading is 80% psychology, 20% strategy."

15.2 Understanding Trading Emotions

Key emotions every trader faces:

1. **Fear**
    - Fear of loss can prevent entry or cause premature exit
2. **Greed**
    - Chasing profit can lead to overtrading or high-risk decisions
3. **Hope**
    - Ignoring stop-loss in hope price will reverse
4. **Regret**
    - Overanalyzing missed opportunities

"Emotions are natural the goal is to manage them, not eliminate them."

15.3 Discipline: Following the Plan

Discipline is the **bridge between strategy and results**:

- Stick to entry and exit rules
- Respect stop-loss and take-profit
- Avoid overtrading or revenge trading

"Discipline transforms knowledge into consistent profits."

15.4 Patience: Waiting for the Right Opportunity

Patience is essential:

- Wait for high-probability setups
- Avoid forcing trades just to be active
- Accept that sometimes **no trade is the best trade**

"Patience in trading is not idleness it's calculated restraint."

15.5 Confidence vs. Overconfidence

- **Confidence:** Trusting your analysis and plan
- **Overconfidence:** Ignoring risk, overleveraging, or deviating from rules

Maintain confidence by **testing strategies and reviewing performance**, not by luck or intuition alone.

15.6 Handling Losses: Learning from Mistakes

Losses are part of trading:

- Review each loss objectively
- Identify what went wrong: strategy, execution, or emotion
- Adjust your plan or approach if needed

"Losses are teachers, not punishers. Learn and move forward."

15.7 Journaling for Mindset Control

Keep a **trading journal** for emotional awareness:

- Record trades, results, and feelings
- Note impulsive decisions or emotional reactions
- Use journal insights to improve both strategy and mindset

"Your journal is a mirror it reflects not just trades but your mental state."

15.8 Visualization and Mental Rehearsal

Top traders use mental exercises:

- Visualize successful trades
- Mentally rehearse difficult scenarios
- Prepare emotionally for losses and volatility

"The mind executes what it believes and rehearses."

15.9 Building a Routine

A disciplined routine strengthens mindset:

- Morning analysis of markets
- Scheduled trading hours
- Breaks and reflection time
- Evening review and journaling

"Routine creates predictability, which reduces emotional mistakes."

15.10 Avoiding External Distractions

- Limit social media or news overload
- Focus on your plan and strategy
- Avoid copying other traders impulsively

"Noise outside the plan is the enemy of calm trading decisions."

15.11 Key Habits for a Strong Trading Mindset

1. Stick to your trading plan consistently
2. Accept losses gracefully
3. Avoid chasing trades
4. Practice emotional awareness
5. Review performance regularly
6. Maintain discipline under pressure

"Habits shape your mindset, mindset shapes your trades, trades shape your success."

15.12 Mindset Exercises

1. **Daily Reflection:** Review trades and emotions
2. **Meditation:** Reduces stress and improves focus
3. **Breathing Exercises:** Control panic during volatile moments
4. **Affirmations:** Reinforce confidence and discipline

"Mindset is like a muscle exercise it daily for strength."

15.13 Avoiding Common Mindset Pitfalls

- Overtrading after wins
- Revenge trading after losses
- Ignoring rules in hope of big profit
- Comparing yourself to other traders

"Your only competitor is yourself focus on improvement, not comparison."

15.14 Integrating Mindset with Strategy

Mindset and strategy are inseparable:

- Strategy gives the roadmap
- Mindset ensures execution
- Discipline, patience, and confidence **turn potential into consistent results**

"Even the perfect strategy fails without the right mindset to implement it."

15.15 Summary: Cultivating a Trader's Mind

A strong trading mindset:

- Accepts losses as part of the game
- Controls fear, greed, and impulsiveness
- Practices patience, discipline, and focus
- Reviews performance and adapts continuously

"Train your mind first, your strategy second, and profits will follow naturally."

The next chapter will focus on **combining technical and fundamental analysis**, showing how to merge price patterns with real-world events for smarter trading decisions.

Chapter 16

Combining Technical &Fundamental Analysis

Introduction: The Power of Integration

Traders often ask: should I use **technical analysis** or **fundamental analysis**? The truth is, both are powerful and when combined, they give a **complete picture of the market**. Technical analysis shows **price trends and patterns**, while fundamental analysis explains **why the market moves.** Together, they allow smarter, higher-probability trades.

This chapter will teach you **how to merge these two approaches** into one cohesive trading strategy.

16.1 Why Combining Both Analyses Matters

Markets are influenced by **data, news, and human psychology**:

- Technical analysis identifies trends, reversals, and setups
- Fundamental analysis explains the underlying reasons for price movement
- Integration increases confidence in trade decisions

"Think of technicals as the map and fundamentals as the compass together they guide you to your destination."

16.2 Technical Analysis Recap

Technical analysis focuses on:

- Price action (candlesticks, trendlines, channels)
- Indicators (moving averages, RSI, MACD)
- Patterns (head & shoulders, triangles, flags)
- Volume and momentum

It answers **"when to enter or exit a trade"** but doesn't explain **why the price moves.**

16.3 Fundamental Analysis Recap

Fundamental analysis focuses on:

- Economic indicators (GDP, inflation, interest rates)
- Company performance (earnings, revenue, balance sheets)
- Industry trends and geopolitical events
- Market sentiment and news

It answers **"why the market is moving"** but doesn't give precise entry or exit timing.

"Fundamentals explain the story; technicals show the behavior."

16.4 Combining Technicals with Fundamentals

Integration creates a **synergy of knowledge and timing**:

1. **Identify opportunities with fundamentals:**
    - Positive earnings reports
    - Strong economic growth indicators
    - Favorable policy announcements
2. **Confirm entry and exit with technicals:**
    - Trendline support/resistance
    - Breakout confirmation
    - Momentum indicators

Example:

- Stock XYZ reports strong quarterly earnings → bullish sentiment
- Technical chart shows breakout above resistance → trade entry confirmed

"Fundamentals point to opportunity; technicals perfect the timing."

16.5 Top Combined Strategies

1. Trend-Following with Fundamentals

- Identify a fundamentally strong asset
- Use technicals to follow upward trend
- Enter on pullbacks, exit near resistance

2. Reversal Trades with Fundamental Catalysts

- Look for fundamentally weak news or overvaluation
- Confirm with reversal candlestick patterns
- Example: Company misses earnings → bearish engulfing forms → short entry

3. Breakout Trades Around News Events

- Key economic report released (e.g., interest rate decision)
- Wait for technical breakout confirmation
- Execute trades with proper stop-loss

"Combine the story and the chart the market rarely lies when both align."

16.6 Practical Example: Stocks

- Company ABC beats revenue expectations → bullish fundamental signal
- Daily chart shows stock breaking ascending triangle → technical confirmation
- Entry: ₹500, Stop-loss: ₹490, Target: ₹550
- Result: Trade aligns with fundamentals, increasing probability of success

16.7 Practical Example: Forex

- U.S. interest rate hike expected → USD strengthens
- EUR/USD trendline shows support break → technical confirmation
- Entry: Short EUR/USD at 1.1000, Stop-loss: 1.1040, Target: 1.0900

"Combining both analyses improves timing and confidence in every market."

16.8 Practical Example: Commodities

- Oil inventory reports show supply shortage → bullish fundamental signal
- Gold futures chart shows breakout above resistance → technical confirmation

- Entry: Buy oil at $80, Stop-loss: $78, Target: $85

16.9 Practical Example: Crypto

- Regulatory clarity on BTC adoption → bullish fundamental signal
- BTC chart shows ascending channel → breakout confirmation
- Entry: $30,000, Stop-loss: $29,000, Target: $32,000

"Even in highly volatile crypto, fundamentals anchor the trade, technicals guide execution."

16.10 Benefits of Combining Both Approaches

1. Higher probability trades
2. Reduced false signals
3. Increased confidence in entries and exits
4. Better adaptation to different market conditions
5. Holistic market understanding

"Technicals tell you what the market is doing; fundamentals tell you why."

16.11 Common Mistakes to Avoid

- Ignoring fundamentals in technical setups → missed context
- Ignoring technicals in fundamental trades → bad timing
- Overanalyzing both → paralysis by analysis
- Overleveraging during news events → unnecessary risk

"Balance is key use fundamentals for direction, technicals for precision."

16.12 Key Takeaways: Integrated Analysis

- Use fundamentals to **identify opportunities**
- Use technicals to **confirm entry and exit**
- Merge both for **higher probability and safer trades**

Review performance to refine your combined

- Strategy "Traders who combine story and chart are prepared, confident, and disciplined."

16.13 Summary: The Complete Market Picture

By integrating **technical and fundamental analysis**:

- You gain a **complete understanding of market moves**
- Reduce impulsive decisions
- Trade with both **knowledge and timing**

The next chapter will focus on **trading plans for beginners vs. advanced traders**, showing how to scale strategies, risk, and mindset for long-term growth.

Chapter 17

Trading Plans for Beginners
vs.
Advanced Traders

Introduction: Trading Plans Evolve With Experience

A trading plan is not static it **evolves as a trader grows.** Beginners require **structured, simple plans** that focus on learning, risk control, and consistency. Advanced traders need **complex, adaptable plans** that integrate multiple markets, strategies, and dynamic risk management.

This chapter explains **how trading plans differ for beginners and advanced traders**, helping you align your plan with your level, experience, and goals.

17.1 Why Trading Plans Change With Experience

- Beginners are learning **market basics, patterns, and discipline**
- Advanced traders focus on **optimization, diversification, and scaling**
- Experience allows for handling complexity, while beginners benefit from simplicity

"A trading plan is like training wheels remove them only when you're ready to ride freely."

17.2 Beginner Trading Plans: Simplicity First

Beginners need plans that **focus on fundamentals**:

1. **Goals**
    - Short-term learning and consistency
    - Focus on small, achievable profits
2. **Trading Style**
    - Simple style like swing trading or position trading
    - Avoid complex multi-strategy approaches
3. **Market Selection**

- One or two markets only (stocks, major forex pairs)

4. **Strategy Rules**
    - One or two strategies
    - Clear entry and exit rules
    - Basic use of indicators like moving averages and RSI
5. **Risk Management**
    - Max 1–2% capital risk per trade
    - Daily and weekly loss limits
6. **Journaling**
    - Record trades, emotions, and mistakes
    - Review weekly for learning

"Beginners should focus on learning discipline, understanding markets, and controlling risk not chasing big profits."

17.3 Advanced Trading Plans: Complexity With Control

Advanced traders handle **larger capital, multiple strategies, and diversified markets**:

1. **Goals**
    - Short-term profit targets + long-term growth
    - Portfolio diversification and risk-adjusted returns
2. **Trading Style**
    - Multiple strategies (trend-following, scalping, swing)
    - Across multiple markets (stocks, forex, commodities, crypto)
3. **Market Selection**
    - Active monitoring of multiple markets
    - Use of correlation and hedging strategies
4. **Strategy Rules**
    - Complex rules using multiple indicators and patterns
    - Entry, exit, and position sizing adjusted per market conditions
5. **Risk Management**
    - Dynamic risk allocation
    - Position scaling

- Portfolio-level risk limits

6. **Automation and Tools**
    - Algorithmic trading or bots
    - Alerts, screening, and analytics tools
7. **Review and Adaptation**
    - Daily, weekly, and monthly performance review
    - Strategy optimization based on results and market conditions

"Advanced plans focus on efficiency, flexibility, and optimization turning experience into measurable results."

17.4 Key Differences Between Beginner and Advanced Plans

Aspect	Beginner Plan	Advanced Plan
Complexity	Simple, single strategy	Multiple strategies and markets
Risk Management	Fixed % per trade	Dynamic, portfolio-level risk
Tools	Basic charts and indicators	Automation, analytics, alerts
Goals	Learning and small profits	Consistent growth and diversification
Review	Weekly review	Daily, weekly, monthly analysis
Flexibility	Stick to one style	Adapt strategies to conditions

"Beginners focus on mastering basics; advanced traders focus on optimizing every variable."

17.5 Transitioning from Beginner to Advanced

Key steps for evolution:

1. **Master the basics**
    - Learn charts, indicators, and a single strategy
2. **Document and review trades**
    - Build discipline and awareness
3. **Gradually add complexity**
    - Introduce new markets, strategies, or position scaling
4. **Develop a flexible mindset**
    - Adapt to market changes without emotional bias
5. **Incorporate technology**
    - Use automation, alerts, and advanced analytics

"Trading is a journey your plan evolves as your skills, experience, and confidence grow."

17.6 Practical Example: Beginner Plan

- Market: Nifty 50 Stocks
- Strategy: Swing trading with moving averages
- Risk: 2% per trade
- Trade log: Record entry, exit, emotion
- Review: Weekly performance evaluation

"Simple, focused, and disciplined the beginner's plan prioritizes learning and consistency."

17.7 Practical Example: Advanced Plan

- Markets: Stocks, Forex, Crypto
- Strategies: Swing trading, scalping, trend-following
- Risk: Dynamic per position, max 5% portfolio loss per week
- Automation: Alerts for multi-market monitoring, algorithmic trade execution
- Review: Daily and weekly analytics with strategy optimization

"Complex, integrated, and adaptive the advanced plan maximizes efficiency and probability of success."

17.8 Common Mistakes in Trading Plans

- Beginners: Overcomplicating strategies, ignoring risk, skipping journaling
- Advanced: Over-leveraging, ignoring simplicity, neglecting discipline
- Both: Not reviewing and adapting the plan regularly

"A plan without review is like a map with no destination it won't take you anywhere."

17.9 Key Takeaways

1. Beginner plans should focus on simplicity, learning, and risk control
2. Advanced plans integrate multiple strategies, markets, and tools

3. Evolution from beginner to advanced requires experience, discipline, and consistent review
4. Both types of plans require journaling, adherence, and emotional control

"Your trading plan grows with you the better your plan, the more consistent your success."

17.10 Summary: Planning for Every Stage

Whether you are a beginner or an advanced trader:

- **Start simple, stay disciplined, and control risk**
- **Add complexity gradually as you gain experience**
- **Review, adapt, and optimize** for continuous growth

The next chapter will focus on **risk management strategies**, showing how to protect capital, scale positions, and survive market volatility.

Chapter 18

Advanced Risk Management Strategies

Introduction: Protecting Your Capital Is Key

In trading, profits are important, but **capital preservation is paramount.** Without proper risk management, even the best strategies fail. Advanced traders understand **how to scale positions, limit losses, and survive market volatility.**

This chapter explores **advanced risk management techniques**, showing how to **trade safely, optimize returns, and stay in the game long-term.**

18.1 Why Advanced Risk Management Matters

Markets are unpredictable. Advanced risk management helps you:

- Avoid catastrophic losses
- Trade consistently under varying market conditions
- Optimize returns without unnecessary risk
- Maintain psychological stability

"Capital preservation is not optional it's the foundation of long-term trading success."

18.2 Risk vs. Reward: The Core Principle

Every trade involves **risk** (potential loss) and **reward** (potential gain). Successful traders balance these:

- Common ratio: **1:2 or 1:3 risk/reward**
- Example: Risk ₹100 to potentially gain ₹200–₹300
- Ensures profitable trades outweigh losing trades over time

"Never risk what you cannot afford to lose, and always aim for more than you risk."

18.3 Position Sizing: Adjusting for Safety

Position sizing determines **how much to invest per trade:**

- Formula: Capital × Risk % ÷ Stop-loss distance
- Adjusts exposure based on volatility and strategy
- Example: If risking 2% of capital, calculate units so stop-loss loss = 2%

"Correct position sizing turns a losing trade into a manageable setback."

18.4 Stop-Loss and Take-Profit Placement

Advanced traders **refine stop-loss and take-profit levels**:

- Use **technical levels**: support/resistance, moving averages
- Adjust dynamically: trailing stop-loss for trends
- Avoid arbitrary percentages; base stops on **market structure**

"A stop-loss is not a restriction it's your insurance against large losses."

18.5 Scaling In and Out of Positions

Scaling allows **flexibility in trade management**:

- **Scaling In:** Enter gradually to reduce risk
- **Scaling Out:** Exit gradually to lock profits
- Adjust based on market conditions and trend strength

Example:

- Buy half position at breakout
- Add remaining if trend confirms
- Exit partial profits at resistance, let rest ride

"Scaling lets you participate without overexposure, improving both safety and potential gains."

18.6 Diversification Across Trades and Markets

Avoid putting all eggs in one basket:

- Trade multiple instruments
- Spread across sectors, asset classes, or markets
- Reduces risk of total portfolio drawdown

"Diversification is a shield it smooths volatility and reduces catastrophic risk."

18.7 Hedging: Protecting Positions

Hedging reduces exposure to adverse moves:

- Use options, futures, or correlated instruments
- Example: Long stock, short index futures to limit market risk
- Effective for protecting gains or reducing volatility

"Hedging is not profit-seeking it's peace of mind in uncertainty."

18.8 Risk Limits: Daily, Weekly, Monthly

Set strict limits to prevent **emotional trading**:

- Daily loss limit: stop trading after a set loss
- Weekly/monthly limits: review performance and adjust
- Helps maintain **psychological discipline and capital protection**

"Limits are not restrictions they are your safety net in volatile markets."

18.9 Volatility-Based Risk Management

Advanced traders adapt to **market volatility**:

- Higher volatility → smaller position sizes
- Lower volatility → larger position sizes
- Use **ATR (Average True Range)** or volatility indicators to adjust stops and size

"Markets fluctuate; your risk management should flex with them."

18.10 Combining Multiple Risk Tools

Top traders combine techniques for maximum protection:

- Position sizing + stop-loss + diversification + hedging
- Example: Swing trade in volatile stock
    - Limit 2% capital per trade
    - Stop-loss at support
    - Partial profit-taking

  - Hedge with index ETF

"Multiple risk tools work like layers of armor one may fail, but others protect you."

18.11 Psychological Risk Management

- Accept losses as part of trading
- Avoid revenge or impulsive trading
- Stick to predefined risk rules
- Maintain emotional stability under pressure

"The strongest risk management tool is a disciplined mind."

18.12 Practical Example: Advanced Risk Management Trade

- Trade: Stock ABC breakout
- Capital: ₹1,00,000
- Risk per trade: 2% → ₹2,000
- Stop-loss: ₹50 below entry → buy 40 shares
- Take-profit: ₹150 above entry, scale out at ₹100 and ₹150
- Outcome: Max loss limited to ₹2,000, profit potential ₹6,000

"With advanced risk rules, losses are controlled and gains optimized."

18.13 Common Mistakes in Risk Management

- Ignoring stop-loss or moving it arbitrarily
- Over-leveraging in volatile markets
- Failing to diversify
- Not adapting to changing market conditions
- Trading emotionally beyond limits

"Even a perfect strategy fails without proper risk management."

18.14 Key Takeaways: Protecting Capital First

1. Always define risk/reward for each trade
2. Use proper position sizing
3. Place stop-loss and take-profit intelligently
4. Scale positions and diversify
5. Hedge when necessary
6. Set strict daily, weekly, monthly limits
7. Adjust for volatility
8. Keep psychological control

"Preserve your capital first profits will follow naturally when risk is managed."

18.15 Summary: The Foundation of Long-Term Trading

Advanced risk management ensures:

- Longevity in trading
- Consistent, steady growth
- Emotional stability under pressure
- The ability to capitalize on opportunities without fear

The next chapter will focus on **developing a trading routine and habit**, showing how structure, repetition, and discipline maximize both profits and mental well-being.

Chapter 19

Developing a Trading Routine and Habit

Introduction: Success Lies in Consistency

Trading is not just about strategy or analysis it's about **discipline, routine, and habits.** The most successful traders don't rely on luck; they follow **structured routines** that maximize focus, consistency, and performance.

This chapter explores **how to create a daily, weekly, and monthly trading routine**, and how to build habits that support long-term success.

19.1 Why Routines and Habits Matter

- Markets are unpredictable, but your behavior shouldn't be
- Routines reduce stress and emotional mistakes
- Habits turn disciplined actions into automatic responses
- Consistency compounds into long-term success

"Good habits are the invisible foundation of profitable trading."

19.2 Morning Routine: Preparing for the Market

A productive trading day begins **before the first trade**:

1. **Market Analysis**
    - Check news, economic reports, and global events
    - Review market sentiment and overnight price action
2. **Technical Scan**
    - Identify support/resistance, trending instruments
    - Flag potential setups for the day
3. **Trading Plan Review**
    - Confirm strategies, risk allocation, and stop-loss levels
4. **Mindset Preparation**
    - Meditation, breathing, or visualization
    - Focus on discipline and patience

"Preparation in the morning sets the tone for disciplined execution all day."

19.3 Trading Session Routine

During market hours:

1. **Follow the Plan**
   - Only take trades that fit your strategy
   - Stick to risk limits and position sizing
2. **Monitor Markets**
   - Watch for opportunities and volatility
   - Avoid impulsive trades or chasing the market
3. **Record Keeping**
   - Note entry, exit, position size, and emotions
   - Helps with learning and review later

"Trading without routine is like sailing without a compass you move, but you drift."

19.4 Evening Routine: Review and Reflection

After the market closes:

1. **Trade Journal Review**
   - Evaluate each trade: what worked, what didn't
   - Identify emotional triggers or mistakes

1. **Strategy Adjustment**
   - Refine rules or setups based on performance
   - Update watchlists for the next day
2. **Mental Reset**
   - Detach from losses and wins
   - Relaxation or meditation to reduce stress

"Reflection turns experience into wisdom without it, mistakes repeat."

19.5 Weekly Routine: Planning Ahead

- Review weekly performance: profits, losses, and risk adherence

- Identify trends or setups for the upcoming week
- Adjust trading plan if necessary
- Set weekly goals for growth and learning

"Weekly routines keep your trading aligned with long-term objectives."

19.6 Monthly Routine: Big Picture Analysis

- Analyze monthly portfolio performance
- Evaluate strategies and market behavior
- Review goals and progress toward long-term objectives
- Plan for the next month, including risk adjustments

"Monthly review ensures your trading evolves, grows, and adapts."

19.7 Building Positive Trading Habits

1. **Discipline**
   - Follow the plan and risk rules consistently
2. **Patience**
   - Wait for high-probability setups
3. **Journaling**
   - Record trades, emotions, and lessons daily
4. **Continuous Learning**
   - Read, watch, or study markets regularly
5. **Emotional Control**
   - Use meditation, breaks, or mindfulness to stay calm

"Habits are automatic behaviors the more positive habits you build, the fewer mistakes you make."

19.8 Breaking Bad Habits

- Avoid overtrading or revenge trading
- Don't ignore stop-loss rules
- Avoid trading out of boredom or stress
- Minimize impulsive decisions caused by greed or fear

"Eliminating bad habits is as important as building good ones it protects both capital and mindset."

19.9 Automation and Reminders

- Set alerts for setups, stop-loss, and profit targets
- Use trading checklists for consistency
- Leverage calendar reminders for reviews and analysis

"Automation supports routine it doesn't replace discipline, but enhances it."

19.10 The Power of Compounding Habits

Consistent routines and habits:

- Reduce mistakes and emotional trading
- Improve execution and efficiency
- Compound small advantages into long-term profitability

*"Success in trading is not about big wins; it's about **small, consistent, disciplined actions repeated daily.**"*

19.11 Practical Daily Trading Routine Example

Morning (Pre-market)

- 30 min news review
- Technical scan of watchlist
- Strategy and risk review
- Mental preparation

Market Hours

- Trade only according to plan
- Stick to stop-losses and position sizing
- Record trades and emotions

Evening (Post-market)

- Journal review

- Strategy reflection and adjustment
- Mental reset

Weekly

- Performance review, goal-setting, and preparation

Monthly

- Portfolio review, strategy refinement, and long-term planning

"A structured routine turns trading from a gamble into a system."

19.12 Key Takeaways: Routine and Habit

1. Start each day prepared with analysis and mindset work
2. Execute trades according to your plan consistently
3. Journal and review every trade
4. Set weekly and monthly goals
5. Build positive habits and eliminate negative ones
6. Leverage reminders and automation to support discipline

"Routine and habit are the scaffolding they hold up your strategy, mindset, and success."

19.13 Summary: Turning Discipline Into Results

A strong trading routine and disciplined habits:

- Reduce mistakes
- Enhance consistency and confidence
- Support long-term growth and profitability

"Master your routine, master your habits, and the market becomes an arena of opportunity rather than stress."

The next chapter will conclude the book with **final thoughts, trading philosophy, and a roadmap for continuous growth**, tying together all previous chapters.

Chapter 20

Final Thoughts and Roadmap for Continuous Growth

Introduction: Trading Is a Journey, Not a Destination

Congratulations! By reaching this chapter, you have explored **trading fundamentals, technical and fundamental analysis, strategies, mindset, risk management, and routines**. But the journey does not end here. Trading is **a lifelong learning process**, where continuous growth, adaptation, and discipline define your success.

This chapter ties together all lessons, offering a **roadmap to keep improving and evolving as a trader.**

20.1 Review of Key Lessons

1. **Trading Basics:** Understanding markets, instruments, and the core principles of buying and selling.
2. **Technical Analysis:** Reading charts, patterns, trends, indicators, and momentum for precise entries and exits.
3. **Fundamental Analysis:** Interpreting news, earnings, economic data, and global events to understand market moves.
4. **Trading Strategies:** Applying strategies across stocks, forex, commodities, and crypto with proper adaptation.
5. **Mindset:** Managing fear, greed, discipline, and patience to maintain consistent trading behavior.
6. **Risk Management:** Protecting capital with stop-loss, position sizing, diversification, and volatility adjustments.
7. **Routine and Habit:** Establishing daily, weekly, and monthly routines that support consistency and long-term growth.

"Each chapter was a building block together, they form the foundation of a successful trading career."

20.2 The Roadmap to Continuous Growth

Step 1: Master the Fundamentals

- Keep revisiting basic concepts, chart reading, and market principles
- Strong fundamentals prevent costly mistakes

Step 2: Practice with Discipline

- Trade small, track every trade, and stick to your plan
- Consistency beats impulsive attempts

Step 3: Expand Knowledge

- Explore new markets, instruments, and strategies
- Read books, watch videos, and learn from experienced traders

Step 4: Optimize Strategies

- Review past trades regularly
- Identify patterns in your wins and losses
- Adjust strategies without compromising discipline

Step 5: Strengthen Mindset

- Continue journaling emotions and trades
- Practice meditation and focus exercises
- Develop patience and resilience

Step 6: Scale Responsibly

- Increase position size gradually as experience and confidence grow
- Always follow risk limits and maintain capital preservation

Step 7: Build Long-Term Habits

- Follow daily, weekly, and monthly routines consistently
- Automate repetitive tasks to focus on high-value decisions
- Keep learning and adapting to market changes

"Growth in trading is gradual patience, discipline, and structured learning compound into long-term success."

20.3 Avoiding Common Pitfalls on the Road Ahead

1. Chasing quick profits or shortcuts
2. Overleveraging or ignoring risk management
3. Ignoring personal emotions or stress
4. Copying others blindly instead of developing your strategy
5. Becoming complacent after short-term success

"Trading is a marathon, not a sprint vigilance and self-awareness are your best tools."

20.4 The Continuous Learning Mindset

- Stay curious about markets and global trends
- Treat every trade as a learning opportunity
- Review failures with a constructive mindset
- Celebrate discipline and consistency, not just profits

"Continuous growth comes from humility, curiosity, and relentless improvement."

20.5 Final Words of Wisdom

- **Capital preservation** comes first without it, opportunities vanish
- **Discipline and routine** create predictability in an unpredictable market
- **Mindset and habits** differentiate successful traders from gamblers
- **Integration of technical and fundamental analysis** increases confidence and probability of success
- **Patience and consistency** are your most powerful allies

"Trading is a skill, an art, and a journey. Your goal is not perfection in one trade, but mastery over your behavior, strategies, and growth over time."

20.6 Your Trading Journey Starts Now

- Begin applying what you've learned gradually
- Maintain small, disciplined trades while reinforcing routines
- Document everything in your journal
- Review, adapt, and grow continuously

"Every successful trader started where you are today curious, motivated, and committed to learning. The market rewards preparation, discipline, and persistence. Start your journey now, and let every trade teach you something new."

20.7 Summary: A Roadmap for Lifelong Trading Success

1. Master the basics → build a strong foundation
2. Develop technical and fundamental analysis skills → understand the market fully
3. Apply strategies wisely → adapt to markets
4. Maintain mindset and discipline → control emotions
5. Implement advanced risk management → protect capital
6. Build routines and habits → reinforce consistency
7. Continuously learn, review, and optimize → evolve as a trader

"The journey of trading is never truly finished but with discipline, knowledge, and patience, your growth and success are limitless."

THE END

www.ingramcontent.com/pod-product-compliance
Lightning Source LLC
LaVergne TN
LVHW090415210926
848480LV00002B/576